CONTENTS

Ships in Focus Publications
Correspondence and editorial:
Roy Fenton
18 Durrington Avenue
London SW20 8NT
020 8879 3527
rfenton@rfenton.demon.co.uk
Orders and photographic:
John & Marion Clarkson
18 Franklands, Longton
Preston PR4 5PD
01772 612855
sales@shipsinfocus.co.uk

Printed by Amadeus Press Ltd., Cleckheaton, Yorkshire.
Designed by Hugh Smallwood, John Clarkson and Roy Fenton.

SHIPS IN FOCUS RECORD
ISBN 1 901703 75 4

SHIPS IN FOC

Noven

Throughout the history of 'Record
record both written and photograpl
and above all ships that have shaped shipping history over the last century and a half. With 28 issues bound into seven volumes, we are conscious that it is getting increasing difficult to find a given ship mentioned in 'Record'. This is a particular problem for the editors who are constantly looking back for such references, and 'Putting the Record Straight' in this issue mentions a glaring example of an editor's failure to do this. After a little gentle prodding from George Robinson, who produces the invaluable index to 'Marine News', we are therefore producing a cumulative index of 'Record' up to issue 28. This is essentially a combination of the indexes which we have included with every fourth issue, but with the important addition of the issue number (an addition which has taken a disproportionate amount of effort). The intention is to produce new cumulative indexes every few years, say after every two of our notional volumes. The index is produced by laser printing, is A4-sized and comes with a cardboard cover, and is available from Ships in Focus, 18 Durrington Avenue, London SW20 8NT £5 post-free (Heather Fenton, who compiled it, will assure you it is worth far more than that). It can also be ordered from our Preston address, if you are buying other books. Indexes will be printed according to demand, so please allow time for your order to be processed. So, George, it's our turn to prod you: when will there be a cumulative index to 'Marine News'?

Opposite are details of the latest books from Ships in Focus. 'Orient Line' should be out when you read this: printing was delayed whilst we waited for some important photographs to arrive. 'SD14: The Full Story' is presently on track to be published in early December. Far from simply being a new edition of the author's 1976 softback on the subject, the SD14 book contains a new account of how the design evolved and grew, and details the career of each ship. There is considerable interest amongst enthusiasts in the few SD14s that survive, and in this issue of 'Record' we include a list of these drawn up by Nigel Jones with the help of David Hazell and Simon Smith. To help keep the SD14 book up to date, we hope to publish such lists at regular intervals.

John Clarkson Roy Fenton

SUBSCRIPTION RATES FOR RECORD

Readers can start their subscription with any issue, and are welcome to backdate it to receive previous issues.

	3 issues	4 issues
UK	£23	£31
Europe (airmail)	£25	£34
Rest of the world (surface mail)	£25	£34
Rest of the world (airmail)	£30	£40

El Uruguayo: see page 8. *[B.Feilden / D.H.Johnzon collection]*

Fleet in Focus
THE FURNESS WITHY - HOULDER BROTHERS LINK
Part 1
D.H. Johnzon

Furness Withy's ambition to become involved in the lucrative trade in frozen and chilled meat imported from Argentina, Chile and Uruguay was realised in 1911 when, though uninvited, the company's F.W. Lewis (later Lord Essendon) attended a meeting of the board of directors of Houlder Bros. and Co. Ltd. It had become known that Houlders faced some difficulties, with share values in decline, no new refrigerated ships added to their fleet since 1902, and their tonnage very recently depleted as part of an agreement; four of its largest units having been sold to the New Zealand Shipping Company upon withdrawal from the Federal-Houlder-Shire Line consortium. To add to the embarrassment, a number of senior directors were in disagreement on future policy.

On behalf of Sir Christopher Furness, F.W. Lewis put forward a generous proposition, and negotiated a settlement there and then. Furness Withy would purchase the shares of the dissident directors, who would be replaced by an equal number of Furness Withy men. Capital would be injected and new ships ordered to boost the existing fleet operated by Houlder Line Ltd. in the River Plate service. The new ships would be registered in the ownership of a jointly owned company to be known as the British and Argentine Steam Navigation Co. Ltd. and, managed by Houlder Brothers, would trade in their livery. Furthermore, the existing fleets of Houlder Line Ltd. and its associate, Empire Transport Co .Ltd., would continue to operate as at present and under those owners' names.

It was an arrangement satisfactory to both parties for not only did it solve Houlders' present problems, but enabled Furness Withy to enter the trade in partnership with a company of considerable experience in the carriage of refrigerated cargoes and highly respected both in the U.K. and in South America.

The Houlder story

At this point a brief history of Houlders will serve to illustrate that company's background and involvement in trade, and its growth in a period lasting some 62 years.

In 1849, Edwin Savory Houlder entered business in London on his own account, as a shipping insurance agent. From 1853, in newly acquired premises, he traded as E.S. Houlder and Co. then in 1856, on taking his elder brother Alfred into partnership, re-styled it Houlder Brothers and Co. With initial concentration on the Australian trade, the company rapidly expanded, now established as shipping and forwarding agents. In 1861 the company acquired its first ship, the tea clipper *Golden Horn*, to be followed by others, entering a service renowned for its regular sailing speed of passage and conveyance, in addition to goods, of passengers in spacious and superior accommodation.

A new phase, together with further expansion, commenced when, in 1881, on a visit to South America, Alfred Houlder signed a contract with the River Plate Fresh Meat Company for the carriage of refrigerated cargo to the U.K. and Continent. It was the first of many, and in the course of time agreements were made with, among others, the Sansinena Meat Company, both Armours and Swift at Ensenada, the port of La Plata; the La Blanca Meat Company; the Soc. Explotadora del Tierra Fuego at Porto Bories, South Patagonia and the Frigorifico Uruguay at Montevideo.

To fulfil early contracts ships were taken on charter. At first owners of vessels required for such purposes were reluctant to go to the expense of fitting refrigeration plant and insulating spaces, and this fell to the forwarding agents. In 1884 the first such shipments reached London on board the steamers *Meath* (2,047/1879) and *Wexford* (2,077/1883) owned by R.M. Hudson and Co. of Sunderland, having loaded at Campana, Argentina. Subsequently a number of larger vessels owned by Turner, Brightman and Co. of London, were chartered under similar arrangements.

In 1888 Houlder Brothers took the decision to operate their own refrigerated vessels, and in 1890 the first pair was delivered, the *Hornby Grange* (2,356gt) in February, and the *Ovingdean Grange* (2,413gt) in March. Unusually for mainly cargo carriers, both were provided with two funnels. Delivered the same year, straight to Buenos Aires by a ship delivery company, were four river steamers; *Apa*, *Asuncion*, *Pilcomayo* and *Rio Paraguay*, each of 433 gross tons, of shallow draft to operate a feeder service to and from up-river plants. Trading in Houlder colours, they were registered in the ownership of the Paraguayan Development Company, formed as a Houlder associate in 1889.

A Houlder office was also opened in Buenos Aires in 1890, to be followed by others at Rosario and Bahia Blanca and later at Montevideo, Uruguay and Santos and Rio de Janeiro in Brazil.

In 1898 Houlder Brothers and Co. was reconstituted to become the limited liability company Houlder Brothers and Co. Ltd. The following year Houlder Line Ltd. was formed and the fleet, now comprising 11 steamers, formerly registered under single ship companies, transferred to its name; Houlder Brothers and Co. Ltd. acting as managers.

The year 1904 saw the construction of the Rio Seco Meat Works at Punta Arenas, Chile in which Houlders held a majority interest. Interest in the Australian and New Zealand route via the Cape had, meanwhile, continued, and in this same year a consortium known as the Federal-Houlder-Shire Line was created to which the Federal Line contributed 11 ships, Turnbull Martin's Elderslie Steamship Co. Shire

Line seven vessels, and Houlder Line four ships - all fully refrigerated. Earlier, during the Boer War, Houlders had played an important part in the provision of remounts shipped to the Cape from the U.K. and Argentina.

Guardiana in Greenland Dock, Surrey Commercial Docks, London. *[E.N.Taylor / D.H.Johnzon collection]*

Furness Withy's first meat carriers

Though ships in the Furness Withy fleets had, periodically, been chartered for Argentine meat cargoes prior to 1906, it seems likely that its interest was further aroused that year upon the formation by Wincett, Cooper and Co. of the Anglo-Argentine Shipping Company, for which two new ships were ordered and, to provide a reasonable service, two others taken on charter. The latter pair included the *Guardiana* (6,852gt) with 397,134 cubic feet of insulated space, which was still under construction and was completed the following year for Furness Withy, and immediate chartered to the new company. She had been laid down as a general cargo vessel for British Maritime Trust. Additionally, Manchester Liner's very first vessel, the *Manchester City* (7,698/1898), was adapted as a refrigerated cargo carrier in 1907.

Manchester City in the Mersey. *[B. & A.Feilden / D.H.Johnzon collection]*

The maritime press of the day waxed lyrically on the attributes of the two identical, handsome looking ships built for Anglo-Argentine by Sir James Laing and Sons Ltd., Sunderland; the *La Blanca* (6,813gt) delivered in December 1906, and the *El Argentino* (6,809gt), completed in February 1907. Attention, in particular, was drawn to the accommodation provided for a limited number of passengers, described by one journalist as 'exceptionally luxurious'. They had been built at a cost of £110,000 each.

Be the above as it may, as early as 12 months after delivery of the *El Argentino* it was clear that the company was unable to meet mortgage repayments. The two ships were accordingly re-possessed, jointly by Sir James Laing and Sons and the builders of the refrigeration plant - J. and E. Hall Ltd. of Dartford, Kent. Towards the end of 1908 the latter bought the former's interest in the vessels and perhaps for the first time a provider of refrigeration machinery became a shipowner in its own right - though briefly.

Early in 1909 J. and E. Hall Ltd., in partnership with Birt, Potter and Hughes Co. Ltd., formed the Argentine Cargo Line Ltd. to continue the operation of these two ships, the latter acting as managers. Then, in 1911 Furness Withy acquired the new company and transferred *La Blanca* and *El Argentino* to the British and Argentine Steam Navigation Co. Ltd. without change of name, and appointed Houlder Brothers to manage them.

The charter of *Guardiana* and *Manchester City* was then concluded. The former returned to Furness Withy and soon afterwards was sold to Houlder Line Ltd. to become their *Sutherland Grange*. Anxious to retain a connection with the South American meat trade, Manchester Liners negotiated separate contracts with meat companies which would enable *Manchester City* still to make periodic voyages to lift refrigerated cargoes in that area. As will be seen, it was a link which would last for a good many years beyond the life of that ship.

New and old reefers for British and Argentine

Five twin-screw, fully refrigerated ships had, meanwhile, been ordered for the British and Argentine Steam Navigation Co. Ltd. Of these, four were delivered in 1912; *El Uruguayo* in April, *El Paraguayo* in June, *La Rosarina* in July and *La Correntina* in December, the *La Negra* following in April 1913. For some unknown reason, 'Lloyd's Register' recorded the *El Uruguayo* as a 1911 ship. A change of mind during the course of construction resulted in *El Paraguayo* and *La Correntina* being completed for Houlder Line Ltd., but without changing their names. With British and Argentine Steam Navigation Co. Ltd. and Houlder Line merged into a single service and, all in Houlder Brothers' livery, there would be little to distinguish one ownership from the other, barring the house flags flown.

To add additional strength to the new combined service, Furness Withy transferred three more ships from their own fleet, placing them under the ownership of the new company. All dated from the turn of the century and the first of these was fully refrigerated with the exception of number 1 hold. She was the *Chaseside*, originally built for T.B. Royden and Co. in 1900 as the *Indradevi*. On transfer she was renamed *El Cordobes* and served in the fleet of the British and Argentine Steam Navigation Co. Ltd. until 1926. The *Oriana*, built in 1902 for the British Maritime Trust and absorbed into the Furness Withy fleet in November 1909, was only partly refrigerated and on transfer retained her name, as did the *Wyandotte,* also with limited refrigeration capacity and built in 1900 as *Lord Roberts*. Thus ten ships were added to a service, which, at this time had been reduced to seven Houlder Line 'Grange' ships, bringing a new total of 17. It was, however, short lived.

In 1914 the *Oriana*, *Wyandotte* and Houlder Line's *Urmston Grange* were sold to other owners, and with the outbreak of the First World War losses through enemy action accounted for four more: *La Correntina* in October 1914, *El Argentino* in 1916, and *La Blanca* and *La Negra* both in 1917.

The most ironic loss was that of *La Correntina* which, at the instigation of Winston Churchill, had been the first of a number of ships to be fitted, in 1913, with defensive armament, comprised of two 4.7 inch guns at the stern. When on 7th October 1914 she was intercepted by the German surface raider *Kronprinz Wilhelm*, she was unable to use them as no shells had been provided. Arrested, she lay helpless, whilst a boarding party transhipped stores and anything useful to the enemy. Even the guns were unshipped and taken across, though without shells they would have proved equally as useless to the Germans. *La Correntina's* crew and passengers were then transferred to a passenger ship - reportedly the *Sierra Nevada* (though this ship is stated elsewhere to have been laid up at Pernambuco from August, 1914) to be landed at Montevideo. No lives had been lost. *La Correntina* was scuttled on October 14th.

Above: *El Paraguayo. [J. & M.Clarkson / D.H.Johnzon collection]*
Below: *La Correntina.* Liverpool, 16th May 1914.
[R.A.Snook / D.H.Johnzon collection]

Above: *Indradevi. [Ian Farquhar collection]*
Below: *Waimarino, ex Wyandotte. [J.Dickie / Ian Farquhar collection]*

Above: *Elstree Grange. [A.Duncan / D.H.Johnzon collection]*
Below: Number 2 hold of the *Abadesa* showing the brine pipes on the deck head for refrigeration purposes. *[D.H.Johnzon collection]*

No photographs have thus far come to light showing the two ex-Argentine Cargo Line ships in Houlder colours, yet their likeness as such can still be seen today in a model housed at Trinity Maritime College, Hull. In pre-Second World War days it was displayed in the window of Houlder's office in Jameson Street, Hull. Fortuitously, as it turned out - since that office was totally destroyed during the devastating blitz on that city - it had been presented to the College in the late 1930s. It bears the name *Leven Grange* - one no doubt intended for a Houlder Line vessel, but never used.

It is worth noting, in passing, that Houlder's established position in Argentina was recognised by the authorities in the U.K. to the extent that, for the duration of the First World War, the company was appointed as British Ministry of Shipping representatives in Buenos Aires. No other company handled so much as a tenth of the number of ships during this period. The amount of work involved proved enormous, and it was as a direct result that premises known as Edificio Houlder were built at 489-499 Calle 25 de Mayo, in the centre of the city and opened in 1922. Further recognition was shown when a mountain in Antarctica was named Mount Houlder by the Shackleton Expedition for valued assistance received prior to setting out on their explorations from Buenos Airea during the war period.

Perhaps partly influenced by anticipated loss to their joint River Plate service, both through enemy action and government service requirements, the two major participants reached a decision in 1915 to order new tonnage and create a new company to operate it. Thus the Furness-Houlder Argentine Line came into being. Orders were placed with various shipyards for five fully refrigerated, twin-screw, 14-knot steamers, of which, owing to the exigencies of wartime requirements, only one was delivered prior to 1918.

In 1916 two vessels were acquired to enable the new company to get under way. The first of these had been under construction for Furness Withy as the *Dominion Miller*. Completed and transferred in March, she was renamed *Abadesa*, and at first had provision for the carriage of frozen meat only in 18 refrigerated spaces (or 'chambers'). In 1929 she was completely refitted and converted from coal to oil burning whilst at the same time being fitted out for loading chilled as well as frozen cargo, the number of spaces so occupied increasing to 44. Acquired by Houlder Line Ltd. she was renamed *Elstree Grange*. As such she served until 3rd May 1941 when, whilst lying in Canada Dock, Liverpool, at the beginning of the Luftwaffe's concentrated attacks upon the city and dock area, she was struck amidships by a parachute mine and totally destroyed. Five of her crew and two shore staff lost their lives.

Bollington Grange at Boston, Mass. 20th June 1915. *[R.Hildebrand / D.H.Johnzon collection]*

Careers of *Canonesa* and *Condesa*

The second acquisition was not unknown to Houlder Brothers. A very odd looking vessel, possessed of two funnels of unequal diameter, she dated back to 1893 when she had been built as the *Buteshire* for Turnbull Martin's Elderslie Steamship Company's Shire Line (see 'Ships in Focus Record' No. 7 page 135), and from 1904 had been among that company's contribution to the Federal-Houlder-Shire Line. Purchased by Houlder Line Ltd. in 1915 she briefly held the name *Bollington Grange*, before being transferred to Furness-Houlder Argentine Lines Ltd. in 1916 and renamed *Canonesa*.

On 1st May 1918 the *Canonesa* was torpedoed off Worthing by the submarine UB 57 with the loss of eight lives. At first it seemed doubtful if she would remain afloat and the master ordered all but a skeleton crew among the survivors to take to three of the ship's four boats. The fourth boat could not be used for, by an extraordinary freak of the torpedo's explosion, it had been blown high above the deck to come to rest atop the broadest of the two funnels. Still holding her own, the ship moved inshore, to be beached on Netley Sands, watched by considerable crowd of people, some among them yelling amusing comments and advice, such as 'Where's your ladder to climb up to that boat, Captain?' 'How do you launch it?' 'Have you got a portable chute tucked away somewhere?'

Abandoned to the government, the ship was ultimately refloated, repaired and virtually rebuilt to be sold to Blue Star Line and renamed *Magicstar*. In her new form she had only one funnel, the donkey boiler steam pipe - represented by the thinner of her former two funnels - led into it. She was sold to shipbreakers in 1929.

In command of the *Canonesa* on her final voyage as such, had been that world-renowned authority on sailing ships, Captain Henry Daniel D.S.C. who, in 1920 was appointed Houlder's Marine Superintendent at Montevideo, a post he held until his retirement in 1954. During the *Graf Spee* episode he additionally acted as a 'Daily Telegraph' correspondent. Later, he took charge of items of special interest to the Admiralty salvaged in a James Bond-type of adventure from the wreck of the *Graf Spee,* supervised the loading of same aboard Furness-Houlder Argentine Line's *Princesa*, including the strengthening of that ship's foredeck to take the weight of an anti-aircraft gun, quite deliberately displayed for the benefit of any watching enemy spies to convince them that therein lay the British interest. The real interest, the radar equipment which had enabled the enemy battleship to score with its 5.9 inch guns such accurate hits upon HMS *Ajax*, *Achilles* and *Exeter*, was secreted below decks in the *Princesa*'s holds. This, together with services rendered gained Captain Daniel an M.B.E.

As earlier indicated, just one of the five new ships on order became available prior to 1918. She was the *Condesa*, which ran trials and was handed over in the closing days of December 1916, ready to commence her maiden voyage on lst January 1917. She was built by Earle's Shipbuilding Co. Ltd. at Hull. She was among the largest ships produced by that yard - and so a search through its listed output reveals - the only Furness Withy vessel built at Hull. Examination of a very detailed general arrangement plan of the ship in the writer's possession makes it plain that far from having been an 'odd one out' the *Condesa* was the forerunner of those which followed, such variations as existed being no greater than as between the four 1918 ships. With a gross tonnage of 8,556, her dimensions were similar and likewise main and refrigeration machinery whilst her capacity of 427,216 cubic feet for refrigerated cargo in 36 chambers, not including trunks, was only marginally less than that of the others.

Sadly, the *Condesa*'s maiden voyage proved to be the only one she would make although, if nothing else, it was protracted. Under the command of Captain W.R. Coleman she sailed from Hull on lst January 1917 and, following a brief call at Plymouth the same day, arrived at Buenos Aires on the 23rd of the month. Loading a full cargo at La Plata she sailed on the 29th bound for Port Natal, presumably under government orders. Though no date of arrival has been traced, a casualty report from Durban advised fire having broken out in the ship's cross bunkers whilst she was lying at Port Natal. Discharge of damaged and burned coal and reloading with adequate fuel, plus minor repairs delayed her sailing until 24th February 1917.

The *Condesa* arrived at Suez on 16th March 1917, sailing for Salonika from Port Said the following day. The length of her stay at Salonika is unknown but she was reported passing southbound through the Suez Canal on the 21st April and arriving back at Buenos Aires on lst June 1917. Here, and probably at La Plata, she again took on a full cargo of refrigerated foodstuffs and on a date unknown set off homeward bound.

At 8.20 pm on Saturday 7th July, on approaching the English Channel, and in position 49.23 north by 08.54 west, the ship was torpedoed by the German submarine U 84 and immediately took on a list, and at 9.00 pm the master ordered all but a skeleton crew to abandon ship. Put in the care of the chief officer, they were straight away picked up by HM Destroyer D 58 which continued to circle the casualty to protect her from further attack. Then, at approximately 10.00 pm, with what seemed to be a strong possibility that the *Condesa* was about to founder, the remainder, comprised of Captain Coleman, the chief and second engineers, first and third officers, radio officer and carpenter, rowed across to HM Yacht *Rovenska* (which from 1920 became Marconi's famous *Electra*) which was standing by. The *Condesa* 's radio having been put out of action by the torpedo explosion, both *Rovenska* and D 58 had sent messages summoning help, emphasising that with immediate tug assistance the ship could probably be saved. During the course of the following night, Captain Coleman's boarding party made several trips across to the ship to examine the latest position, but had decided that nothing could be done until daylight.

At 7.00 am on Sunday 8th July the first response to calls for help was received via Lands End advising that two tugs had put out but had been obliged to return owing to very heavy weather. In fact, it had remained calm, or boat work would not have been possible. During the course of Sunday several attempts were made, first by the small passing tug *Whitefriars*, and later by *Rovenska*, to take the ship in tow, but without success.

It was midday on Monday 9th July before the *Triton*, a large tug from Falmouth, put in an appearance. The boarding party once again returned to the ship to assist with making it fast, but had barely left her when, at 1.30 pm. the hatch covers of numbers 2 and 3 holds blew off and she began to founder, finally disappearing at 2.40 pm in position 49.30 north by 06.34 west to which she had drifted since being torpedoed.

Landed at Falmouth, Captain Coleman at once sought an explanation for the delay in sending help, and learned the astonishing fact that it had resulted from a dispute between the Falmouth tug boat captains as to which of them should have taken duty on the Saturday night and Sunday. Furthermore, it transpired, the *Triton* had only put out that morning on the promise of Sunday pay for master and crew. Bloody mindedness plus sheer greed had led to the loss of a valuable new ship and her awaited cargo.

[To be continued]

Notes on the fleet list

This follows the usual format for Ships in Focus publications, with some extra data. Following the vessel's registered length, are given lengths of forecastle (F), bridge deck (B) and poop (P) if applicable. The type of refrigeration equipment fitted, with the makers, is listed, with the refrigerated capacity and number of spaces. There are variations from year to year in the refrigerated capacities quoted in 'Lloyd's Register, and the smallest and largest capacities are quoted. Where the differences are significant, it can be concluded that the ship at first had provision only for carriage of frozen meat, with facilities for chilled beef being added later. This is reflected in the growth in the number of spaces (or chambers) quoted, since trunk decks are available for chilled meat, and are counted as separate chambers.

1. LA BLANCA 1911-1917

O.N. 124026 Call sign: HJST 6,813g 4,405n 425.0 x 57.3 x 39.0 feet (B: 154 feet)
12 first class passengers plus 336 in 'tween decks.
T. 3-cyl. by George Clark Ltd., Sunderland; 29½, 50, 80 x 54 inches; 12 knots.
Refrigeration equipment: two Duplex carbon dioxide/brine/charcoal and air by J. and E. Hall Ltd., Dartford, Kent; 351,000 cubic feet in 12 chambers.
12.1906: Completed by Sir James Laing and Sons Ltd., Deptford Yard, Sunderland (Yard No. 617) for Anglo-Argentine Shipping Co. Ltd. (Wincett, Cooper and Co. Ltd.), Liverpool as LA BLANCA.
1908: Repossessed jointly by Sir James Laing and Sons Ltd. and J. and E. Hall Ltd.
1908: Owners became J. and E. Hall Ltd., Dartford, Kent; having acquired the shares of Sir James Laing and Sons Ltd.
1909: Sold to Argentine Cargo Line Ltd. (Birt, Potter and Hughes Ltd.), London.
1911: Acquired by British and Argentine Steam Navigation Co. Ltd. (Houlder Brothers and Co. Ltd.) (Transferred by Furness Withy and Co. Ltd. following their purchase of the Argentine Cargo Line Ltd.)
3.1917: During her third survey, gross tonnage increased to 7,479 as a closed shelter decker, and cubic capacity for frozen and chilled cargo increased to 414,204 cubic feet in 14 chambers.
23.11.1917: Torpedoed and sunk (reputedly by U 96), with the loss of two lives, off Berry Head, Devonshire, when nearing the end of a voyage with frozen meat and general for Le Havre.
Total service: 11 years.

La Blanca in Gallions Reach, River Thames 29th April 1914. *[R.A.Snook / D.H.Johnzon collection]*

2. EL ARGENTINO (1) 1911-1916
O.N. 1124040 Call sign: HKFC
6,809g 4,411n 425.0 x 57.3 x 39.0 feet (B: 154 feet)
12 first class passengers plus 336 in 'tween decks.
T. 3-cyl. by George Clark Ltd., Sunderland; 29½, 50, 80 x 54 inches; 12 knots.
Refrigeration equipment: two duplex carbon dioxide/brine/charcoal and air by J. and E. Hall Ltd., Dartford, Kent; 351,000 cubic feet in 12 chambers.
2.1907: Completed by Sir James Laing and Sons Ltd., Deptford Yard, Sunderland (Yard No. 618) for Anglo-Argentine Shipping Co. Ltd. (Wincett, Cooper and Co. Ltd.), Liverpool as EL ARGENTINO.
1908: Repossessed jointly by Sir James Laing and Sons Ltd. and J. and E. Hall Ltd.
1908: Owners became J. and E. Hall Ltd., Dartford, Kent; having acquired the shares of Sir James Laing and Sons Ltd.
1909: Sold to Argentine Cargo Line Ltd. (Birt, Potter and Hughes Ltd.), London.
1911: Acquired by British and Argentine Steam Navigation Co. Ltd. (Houlder Brothers and Co. Ltd., managers), London. (Transferred by Furness Withy and Co. Ltd. following their purchase of the Argentine Cargo Line.)
26.5.1916: Mined and sank seven miles south east by south from Southwold whilst on a voyage in ballast from Hull for London to load for Buenos Aires.
Total service: 9¼ years

Captain R.A. Smiles had the misfortune to be in command of both the above ships at the time of their respective losses. Eleven years later, he took the second EL ARGENTINO on her maiden voyage.

3. EL URUGUAYO 1912-1937
O.N. 132817 Call sign: HVMT (GCSQ from 1934) 8,361g 4,967n 439.9 x 58.8 x 35.7 feet (F: 34 feet, B: 135 feet).
12 first class passengers.
Two T.3-cyl. by Alexander Stephen and Sons Ltd., Glasgow driving twin screws; each 25, 42½, 70 x 48 inches; 13 knots.
Refrigeration equipment: carbon dioxide/brine/cork by J. and E. Hall Ltd., Dartford, Kent; 416,483 cubic feet in 33 chambers.
4.1912: Completed by Alexander Stephen and Sons Ltd., Glasgow (Yard No. 447) for the British and Argentine Steam Navigation Co. Ltd. (Houlder Brothers and Co. Ltd., managers), London as EL URUGUAYO.
30.5.1917: Chased by German submarine off north west coast of Ireland. Escaped by accurate return gunfire.
2.12.1917: A torpedo fired at the ship when in the English Channel missed its target.
1933: Transferred to Furness-Houlder Argentine Lines Ltd. (Houlder Brothers and Co. Ltd., managers), London.
1937: Sold to John Cashmore for £27,000 and broken up at Newport, Monmouthshire
Total service: 25 years.

EL PARAGUAYO (8,508g) was a sister ship of the above, delivered to Houlder Line Ltd. by Irvine's Shipbuilding and Dry Dock Co. Ltd., West Hartlepool and registered in London during June 1912 (see text).

El Argentino. [E.N.Taylor / D.H.Johnzon collection]

El Uruguayo, 24th May 1935. *[F.W.Hawks / J. & M.Clarkson collection]*

El Uruguayo, River Mersey. *[J. & M. Clarkson / D.H.J.ohnzon collection]*

Above: *La Rosarina* sailing from Liverpool. *[D.H.Johnzon collection]*
Below: *La Rosarina* sailing from Liverpool for Japan as *Rosarina*. *[B. & A.Feilden / J. & M.Clarkson collection]*

4. LA ROSARINA 1912-1937
O.N. 132823 Call sign: HWFT (GKRJ from 1934) 8,332g 4,948n 440.0 x 58.8 x 35.7 feet (F: 35 feet, B:135 feet).
12 first class passengers.
Two T. 3-cyl. by Palmers Co. Ltd., Newcastle-on-Tyne driving twin screws; each 25, 41½, 70 x 48 inches; 13 knots.
Refrigeration equipment: carbon dioxide/brine/cork, felt and silicate cotton by J. and E. Hall Ltd., Dartford, Kent; 400,903 cubic feet in 22 chambers.
7.1912: Completed by Palmers Shipbuilding Co. Ltd., Jarrow-on-Tyne (Yard No. 812) for British and Argentine Steam Navigation Co. Ltd. (Houlder Brothers and Co. Ltd., managers), London as LA ROSARINA.
3.11.1914: Arrived at Liverpool from Tenerife with a large number of members of crews of ships sunk by the German raider KARLSRURE, who had been taken into Tenerife by the Norddeutscher Lloyd ship CREFELD.
17.4.1915: Chased by a German submarine off Southern Ireland. Escaped with use of her defensive gun.
6.1.1917: Attacked with gunfire by a surfaced German submarine off Ushant. Returned fire with accuracy and made good her escape.
1933: Transferred to Furness-Houlder Argentine Lines Ltd. (Houlder Brothers and Co. Ltd., managers), London.
1937: Renamed ROSARINA for voyage to shipbreakers, having been sold through London agents to Japanese breakers.
11.9.1937: Sailed from Liverpool for Osaka with a Japanese crew.
1938: Broken up at Osaka.
Total service: 26.years.

In addition to accommodation for 12 first class passengers, this group of ships had provision for emigrants and could accommodate up to 400 in steerage-type quarters in the 'tween decks. On some outward voyages they called at Spanish ports where emigrants boarded for Argentina. Thus on the homeward voyage in November 1914, the LA ROSARINA could cope with the survivors from vessels sunk by the raider KARLSRUHE.
LA CORRENTINA 8,529g, a similar ship to numbers 3 and 4, was delivered to Houlder Line Ltd. in December 1912 by Irvines Shipbuilding and Dry Dock Co. Ltd., West Hartlepool, and registered at Liverpool (see text).

5. EL CORDOBES 1912-1926
O.N. 110639 Call sign: REWY
5,683g 3,702n 420.0 x 53.2 x 29.4 feet (flush decked).
Strengthened deck abreast number 3 hatch for the carriage of railway locomotives and rolling stock.
T. 3-cyl. by J. Dickinson and Sons Ltd., Sunderland; 27, 46, 76 x 51 inches; 11 knots.
Refrigeration equipment: carbon dioxide/brine/charcoal by J. and E. Hall Ltd., Dartford, Kent; 206,905 cubic feet in five chambers, 218,293 cubic feet in six chambers.
3.1900: Completed by Sir James Laing and Sons Ltd., Sunderland (Yard No. 573) for the Indradevi Steamship Co. Ltd. (T.B. Royden and Co., managers), Liverpool as INDRADEVI.
1911: Sold to Furness Withy and Co. Ltd., West Hartlepool and renamed CHASESIDE.
1912: Acquired by the British and Argentine Steam Navigation Co. Ltd. (Houlder Brothers and Co. Ltd., managers), London and renamed EL CORDOBES.
1926: Sold to M. Querci and O. Rosini, Genoa, Italy and renamed PRATOMAGNO.
30.4.1931: Arrived Savona to be broken up.
Total service: 31 years.

6. ORIANA 1912-1914
O.N. 115137 Call sign: TPOK
4,419g 2,882n 382.0 x 48.1 x 28.0 feet (flush decked).
T. 3-cyl. by Richardsons, Westgarth and Co. Ltd., Hartlepool; 25, 41, 69 x 48 inches; 8½ knots.
Refrigeration equipment: carbon dioxide/brine/charcoal by J. and E. Hall Ltd., Dartford, Kent;
47,240 cubic feet in two chambers (as ORIANA); 67,940 cubic feet in four chambers (as JAVA MARU until 1923).
8.1902: Completed by Northumberland Shipbuilding Co. Ltd., Newcastle-on-Tyne (Yard No. 94) for British Maritime Trust Ltd., London (Furness Withy and Co. Ltd., West Hartlepool, managers) as ORIANA.
11.1909: Transferred to Furness Withy and Co. Ltd., West Hartlepool.
1912: Acquired by the British and Argentine Steam Navigation Co. Ltd. (Houlder Brothers and Co. Ltd., managers), London.
1914: Sold to Osaka Shosen Kabushiki Kaisha, Osaka, Japan and renamed JAVA MARU (4,636g)
1923: Refrigeration equipment removed.
1.1925: Sold to Chutaro Nakano (Nachida Shokai, manager), Amino, Japan.
1927: Sold to Tachibana K.K., Fushiki, Japan.
1932: Sold to shipbreakers and dismantled in third quarter of the year.
Total service: 30 years.

El Cordobes. [D.H.Johnzon collection]

El Cordobes. [Raul Maya / D.H.Johnzon collection]

Oriana. [D.H.Johnzon collection]

7. WYANDOTTE 1912-1914
O.N. 110517 Call sign: RNMK
4,204g 2,712n 375 x 48.5 x 27.9 feet (F: 33 feet, B: 86 feet, P: 28 feet).
T. 3-cyl. by Muir and Houston Ltd., Glasgow; 26, 43, 72 x 48 inches; 10 knots.
Refrigeration equipment: one single and one duplex, carbon dioxide/brine/charcoal by J. and E. Hall Ltd., Dartford, Kent; 65,940 cubic feet in four chambers.
4.1900: Completed by A. McMillan and Son Ltd., Dumbarton (Yard No. 369) for Irish Shipowners Ltd. (T. Dixon and Sons, managers), Belfast as LORD ROBERTS.
1900: Sold to British Maritime Trust Ltd., London (Furness Withy and Co. Ltd., West Hartlepool, managers) and renamed WYANDOTTE.
11.1909: Transferred to Furness Withy and Co. Ltd., West Hartlepool.
1912: Acquired by British and Argentine Steam Navigation Co. Ltd. (Houlder Brothers and Co. Ltd., managers), London.
1914: Sold to Union Steamship Co. of New Zealand Ltd., Wellington, New Zealand and renamed WAIMARINO, remaining registered in London. Opened new owner's trans-Pacific cargo service.
7.8.1917: Taken on Government service for cargo of wheat from Pacific Coast states to U.K.
13.12.1917: Service as Royal Navy Collier No. 1941 until 31.1.1918.
1.2.1918: Further wheat cargo voyage, to Argentina for U.K.
15.5.1918: Reverted to Royal Navy Collier No. 1941.
31.8.1918: A voyage for wheat to Karachi, during course of which attacked by submarine in the Mediterranean with a torpedo which missed.
31.8.1925: Laid up at Sydney, New South Wales.
1926: Sold to Chun Young Zan (Moller and Co., managers), Shanghai and renamed KING SING.
1929: Transferred to Moller and Co., Shanghai and renamed DAISY MOLLER.
1934: At first reported that the ship had been broken up at Shanghai, but it subsequently transpired that she was sold to Japanese shipbreakers and dismantled in the first quarter of the year.
Total service: 34years.

Waimarino. [J.Dickie / Ian Farquhar collection]

8. LA NEGRA 1913-1917
O.N. 132839 Call sign: JBWP
8,312g 4,949n 440.2 x 58.8 x 35.7 feet (F: 35 feet, B: 135 feet).
12 first class passengers plus 400 steerage.
Two T. 3-cyl. by Palmers Company Ltd., Newcastle-on-Tyne driving twin screws; each 25, 41½, 70 x 48 inches; 13 knots.
Refrigeration equipment: carbon dioxide/brine/silicate cotton, by J. and E. Hall Ltd., Dartford, Kent; 395,400 cubic feet in 22 chambers.
4.1913: Completed by Palmers Shipbuilding Co. Ltd., Jarrow-on-Tyne (Yard No. 813) for the British and Argentine Steam Navigation Co. Ltd. (Houlder Brothers and Co. Ltd., managers), London as LA NEGRA.
3.9.1917: Torpedoed by submarine UC 50 at 12.15pm and again at 3.12 pm with the loss of 4 lives in the second attack. She was in a position between Ushant and the Casquets, approximately 50 miles south south west from Start Point on a voyage from Buenos Aires for the U.K. with a cargo of frozen meat. At 8.00 pm. she was taken in tow but sank at 2.30 am the following morning in position 49.29 north by 03.52 west.
Total service: 4 years.

La Negra. [D.H.Johnzon collection]

9. CANONESA (1) 1916-1918 Two funnels
O.N. 102653 Call sign: NGJL
5,583g 3,619n 420.0 x 54.0 x 28.7 feet (F: 49 feet, B: 262 feet, P: 41 feet).
12 first class passengers. As completed had provision for 320 third-class emigrant passengers in the 'tween decks.
T. 3-cyl. by Hawthorn, Leslie and Co. Ltd., Newcastle-on-Tyne; 29, 46¼, 75½ x 54 inches; 12 knots.
Refrigeration equipment: two single ammonia/air/pumice and charcoal by Linde British Co. Ltd.; 284,000 cubic feet in eight chambers.
12.1893: Completed by Hawthorn, Leslie and Co. Ltd., Newcastle-on-Tyne (Yard No. 316) for the Elderslie Steamship Co. Ltd. (Turnbull, Martin and Co., managers), Glasgow as BUTESHIRE.
1894: Disabled by loss of propeller. Towed to Mauritius by STRATHORD (4,040/1894, Burrell and Son, Glasgow), a new ship completed in August 1894 which puts this incident late in the year, though exact date unknown.
1904: Allocated to the Federal-Houlder-Shire Line consortium.
1910: Owners re-styled Scottish Shire Line (Turnbull, Martin and Co., managers), Glasgow.
1915: Sold to Houlder Line Ltd. (Houlder Brothers and Co. Ltd., managers), London and renamed BOLLINGTON GRANGE.
2.7.1915: Encountered a submarine about 20 miles north west true of Ushant when on a voyage from Boston, Mass. for Dunkerque with 2,800 tons of frozen meat for the French army. Captain W.H. Brodie ordered helm hard to port, putting enemy astern and sent out an S.O.S. call. The destroyer HMS MASTIFF, which had recently circled the ship, answered the call and put paid to the submarine's interest.
1916: Transferred to Furness-Houlder Argentine Lines Ltd. (Houlder Brothers and Co. Ltd., managers), London and renamed CANONESA.
1.5.1918: Torpedoed off Worthing, Sussex by the German submarine UB 57 with the loss of eight lives. Beached on Netley Sands. Abandoned to the British Government. Subsequently refloated and repaired; being rebuilt with a single funnel.
1919: Sold to Brodway Steam Ship Co. Ltd. (Blue Star Line Ltd., managers), London and renamed MAGICSTAR; call sign now KDRV.
1920: Transferred to Union Cold Storage Co. Ltd. (Blue Star Line Ltd., managers), London.
1929: Sold to shipbreakers and dismantled at Inverkeithing in third quarter of the year.
Total service: 35½ years.

Magicstar. [Tom Rayner / D.H.Johnzon collection]

10. ABADESA (1) 1916-1929
O.N. 137495 Call sign: JMLD
6,572g 4,223n 420.0 x 53.5 x 36.8 feet (F: 34 feet).
T. 3-cyl. by Richardsons, Westgarth and Co. Ltd., Middlesbrough (Engine No. 2232); 29, 49, 80 x 54 inches; 14 knots.
Refrigeration equipment: one duplex carbon dioxide/brine/silicate cotton by J. and E. Hall Ltd., Dartford, Kent; 390,018 cubic feet in 18 chambers (frozen only).
3.1916: Completed by Sir Raylton Dixon and Co. Ltd., Middlesbrough (Yard No. 590) for Furness-Houlder Argentine Lines Ltd. (Houlder Brothers and Co. Ltd., managers), London as ABADESA.
10.1928: Re-engined and converted from coal to oil burning. Gross

Elstree Grange. [J. & M.Clarkson / D.H.Johnzon collection]

tonnage increased to 6,598. Fitted for the carriage of chilled, in addition to frozen, meat, reducing the cubic capacity of refrigerated space by 17,106 to 372,912, stowed in 30 chambers (18 plus 12 trunkways). Also reduced was the ship's speed, the new machinery only capable of propelling her at 12½ knots.
1929: Transferred to Houlder Line Ltd. (Houlder Brothers and Co. Ltd., managers), London and renamed ELSTREE GRANGE retaining Liverpool registration.
16.7.1937: In collision at Punta Indio Channel Buoy No. 281 in the River Plate with Prince Line's SOUTHERN PRINCE (10,917/1929) with considerable damage to both ships.
3.5.1941: Struck amidships by a parachute mine whilst berthed in Canada Dock, Liverpool at the beginning of a series of intensive raids upon city and dockland. The explosion and subsequent detonation of ammunition for her guns reduced the ship to a mass of twisted metal. The chief and fifth engineers, the second officer, an assistant steward and a galley boy, together with a shore watchman and a shore donkeyman, lost their lives. Two seriously wounded members of the crew were rescued in a remarkable feat of bravery on the part of A.B. George Wheeley for which he was later awarded the George Medal.
14.5.1941: Wreck towed out into the river and beached alongside King's Dock wall.
10.1942: Wreck broken up.
Total service: 25 years.

11. CONDESA (1) 1916-1917
O.N. 137531 Call sign: JNRC 8,556g 5,417n 430.6 x 61.1 x 38.4 feet (B: 254 feet).
Two T.3-cyl. by Earle's Shipbuilding and Engineering Co. Ltd., Hull driving twin screws; each 25, 41½, 70 x 48 inches; 14½ knots.
Refrigeration equipment: two engines (No. 15¼ S.M.T. type) carbon dioxide/brine/cork and silicate cotton by J. and E. Hall Ltd., Dartford, Kent.
Refrigerated capacities: a) in the shipbuilder's general arrangement plan: 427,216 cubic feet in 36 chambers including trunks;
(b) in the 1916/1917 edition of 'Lloyd's Register': 432,600 cubic feet in 28 chambers
(c) in the 1918/1919 edition of 'Lloyd's Register': 457,900 cubic feet in 44 chambers.
12.1916: Earle's Shipbuilding and Engineering Co. Ltd., Hull (Yard No. 611) for Furness-Houlder Argentine Lines (Houlder Brothers and Co. Ltd., managers), Liverpool as CONDESA.
1.1.1917: Left on maiden voyage under Captain W.R. Coleman: Hull, Plymouth, Buenos Aires, La Plata, Port Natal (delayed by fire in cross bunkers), Suez, Port Said, Salonica, Suez Canal, Buenos Aires thence homeward bound.
7.7.1917: Torpedoed by the German submarine U 84 in number 3 hold and disabled, in position 49.23 north by 08.54 west at 8.20 pm whilst on a voyage from Buenos Aires to Liverpool with a cargo of frozen meat. At 9.00 pm, with ship listing to starboard and down by the head, all except a skeleton crew taken off by the destroyer D.58, which continued to circle casualty toprevent further attack. Master and skeleton crew taken aboard HM yacht ROVENSKA at 10.00 pm, but made repeated reboardings over the next 40 hours in endeavours to save the ship, during which ROVENSKA continued to stand by. On the following day (Sunday) ROVENSKA, aided by small passing tug, WHITEFRIARS, attempted a tow but without success. Despite repeated calls for assistance none was forthcoming due to a dispute between tug masters.
9.7.1917: Tug TRITON from Falmouth reached casualty at midday and made fast. At 1.30 the ship's hatch covers at numbers 2 and 3 holds blew off and she commenced to founder, disappearing at 2.40 pm in position 49.30 north by 06.54 west. There had been no loss of life among her 93 crew.
Total service: seven months.

[To be continued]

Condesa sinking 9th July 1917. *[Above: Jack Looney / D.H.Johnzon collection, below: World Ship Photo Library / D.H.Johnzon collection]*

RETURN TO THE MERSEY: ALBATROS AND APOLLON

Paul Boot

Following the visit of the *Queen Elizabeth 2* in 1990, Liverpool experienced a minor renaissance as a liner port. Amongst the handful of cruise ships which were to call in the closing years of the last millennium were two steam-turbine powered liners that had each had a long association with the port many years before. Both of these have recently been broken up in India and this portfolio records the early and final years of their careers.

Sylvania (21,989/1957) was the last of four sisters built by John Brown and Co. (Clydebank) Ltd. for Cunard and had operated on the company's Transatlantic services from Liverpool until the end of 1966. After being transferred to Southampton she was sold in 1969, together with *Carinthia*, to Vlasov's Sitmar Line, renamed *Fairwind* and extensively rebuilt. She later became *Sitmar Fairwind* and following the sale of Sitmar's passenger fleet to P&O, she joined the Princess Cruises' fleet as *Dawn Princess*. In 1992 she returned to the Vlasov group and took her final name *Albatros* under the flag of Bahamas. She was to make her one and only return visit to the Mersey on 13th May 1997 on a round Britain cruise when under a long-term charter to the German tourist company Phoenix Reisen. After a day of very changeable weather she departed in glorious sunlight, triumphantly demonstrating on her horn that she was still very much a steamer. Having reportedly experienced engine problems she was withdrawn from service at the end of 2003, and renamed *Genoa* she made her way to Alang arriving on 6th January 2004. *[Above: Paul Boot, opposite: Peter Newall collection]*

In 1998 Direct Holidays started a cruise service running from Liverpool and other British ports during the summer months and took on charter the Greek flagged *Apollon* (28,574/ 1961) from Marianne Shipping Inc., part of Royal Olympic Cruise Line. As *Empress of Canada* she had last visited the Mersey in 1971 when she ended Canadian Pacific's passenger service sixty five years after it had been inaugurated. The following year she was acquired by Ted Arrison and as *Mardi Gras* she became Carnival Cruises Lines' first ship. In 1993 she was sold to Epirotiki Steamship Nav. Co. S.A. and renamed *Star of Texas* in the registered ownership of Seaways Maritime Co. Two years later a change of ownership within the group saw her renamed *Apollon* which, apart from a brief spell in 2000 as *Olympic 2004*, she carried for the rest of her days. Despite her many identities, she remained little changed externally, the most obvious alteration being the removal of pairs of kingposts fore and aft. This view of her arriving at Liverpool on 25th September 1999 from a cruise to the Atlantic Isles, Spain and Portugal records what was to be her penultimate visit to what had been her home port for many years. Although Direct Cruises had a programme of sailings for 2000, these were cancelled before the season had begun and *Apollon* went into lay-up at Piraeus broken only by a brief spell as an accommodation ship. With many of the older cruise liners now being despatched to the breakers, *Apollon's* departure for Alang was inevitable arriving there on 4th December 2003. *[Above: Paul Boot, opposite: Peter Newall collection)*

SPYING ON SPAIN: 3

This is a selection of photographs of Naviera Aznar ships from a collection put together by British intelligence during 1943 and 1944. All the ships were originally owned by Compania Naviera Sota y Aznar of Bilbao, a port in the Basque country. Many Basques were fiercely antagonistic to the right-wing Nationalist cause, and the de la Sota family preferred exile to living under Franco's brutal fascist regime. Hence, at the end of the Spanish Civil War, the ships were returned to the Aznar part of the old partnership and given 'Monte' names in place of their previous Basque names. The original prints, although of high quality, are rather closely cropped.

MONTE AMBOTO
Compania Euskalduna de Const. Bilbao; 1929, 2,955gt, 335 feet
Oil engines 4-cyl. 2SCSA by Sulzer Brothers, Winterthur, Switzerland
A relatively rare motor ship in the Spanish fleet, the *Amboto-Mendi* was taken over by the Nationalist rebels when she arrived at Pasajes from Antwerp in August 1937. She was restored to the Aznar fleet as *Monte Amboto*. Like so many Spanish ships, she had a long life, and was not broken up until late in 1976, at Santander. The photograph is dated 9th July 1944. At least four Spanish flags are painted on the hull, and she carries floats at both masts.

MONTE BUSTELO
William Gray and Co. Ltd., West Hartlepool; 1928, 1,597gt, 280 feet
T. 3-cyl. by Central Marine Engine Works, West Hartlepool
In contrast to *Andutz-Mendi* above, the same company's *Aralar-Mendi* was laid up at Hull from September 1937, returning to service only in 1939 as *Monte Bustelo*. She was broken up at Bilbao in December 1961. Her photograph was taken on 16th July 1944.

MONTE BUITRE
William Gray and Co. Ltd., West Hartlepool; 1929, 1,597gt, 280 feet
T. 3-cyl. by Central Marine Engine Works, West Hartlepool
The Spanish Civil War was particularly hard on *Andutz-Mendi* of Compania Naviera Sota y Aznar. On 29th July 1937 she was heavily damaged by the Nationalist submarine *General Sanjurjo* off Barcelona, and was later sunk during an air raid on Barcelona. Refloated in February 1940 she was rebuilt, lengthened and renamed *Monte Buitre*. She survived until broken up in August 1962. Photographed on 9th July 1944, the significance of the large flag flown from the foremast is not known.

MONTE CASTELO
Compania Euskalduna de Const. Bilbao; 1921, 3,222gt, 335 feet
T. 3-cyl. by Blair and Co. Ltd., Stockton-on-Tees
Arnotegi-Mendi was captured by Nationalists in Bilbao in 1937, although not renamed *Monte Castelo* until 1939. She was broken up at Santander 1964. A Gibraltar-based aircraft photographed her carrying a timber deck cargo on 14th June 1944. Blair and Co. seem to have found favour with Spanish owners and builders: four of the ships in this selection had machinery from this Stockton-on-Tees company.

MONTE FACHO
Compania Euskalduna de Const .y Rep. De Buques, Bilbao; 1910, 3,234gt, 320 feet
T. 3-cyl. by Blair and Co. Ltd., Stockton-on-Tees
Bizkargi-Mendi was laid up at Cardiff from August 1937 until 1939. She is seen as *Monte Facho* on 9th July 1944 with a partial deck cargo of timber. *Monte Facho* was sunk in a collision in fog with the British steamer *Granford* (7,087/1944) in October 1952, some 50 miles off the coast of Portugal.

MONTE ICIAR
Ropner Shipbuilding and Repairing Co. (Stockton) Ltd., Stockton-on-Tees; 1922, 3,303gt, 340 feet
T. 3-cyl. by Blair and Co. Ltd., Stockton-on-Tees
The intervention of Germany and Italy, with relatively well-equipped forces, materially helped the rebel Nationalist cause in the Spanish Civil War. The Governments of the major European democracies - Britain and France - claimed to be neutral but if anything their neutrality helped Franco, although many of their citizens joined the International Brigade to bravely support the Republican cause. Part of the help given by Germany was in re-registering under their flag a number of ships serving the Nationalist cause, giving them some protection from attack by Republicans. *Aizkarai-Mendi* was put under the German flag as *Blanca* in July 1936, and further renamed *Erica* in 1937. A brief return to her former name in 1938 was followed by renaming *Monte Iciar* in 1939, as which she lasted until broken up at Santander in 1963. The photograph dates from 9th July 1944, when she was stopped by a Royal Naval boarding party, whose boat is alongside.

MONTE GALERA
Compania Euskalduna de Const., Bilbao; 1921, 3,222gt, 335 feet
T. 3-cyl. by Blair and Co. Ltd., Stockton-on-Tees
Mussolini's government also allowed Nationalist ships to be registered under nominees, *Artxanda-Mendi* becoming the *Siena* from 1936 to 1939, when she returned to the Spanish flag as *Monte Galera*. She was photographed ghosting into port during June 1943.

Unusually, she was to carry a further name beyond Aznar ownership, being sold to Gijon owners in 1962 as *Cimadevilla*. She was broken up at Bilbao 1968

MONTE JATA
William Gray and Co. Ltd., West Hartlepool; 1909, 4,126gt, 365 feet
T. 3-cyl. by Central Marine Engine Works, West Hartlepool
Eretza-Mendi was captured by the Nationalist auxiliary cruiser *Ciudad De Valencia* in the Bay of Biscay in March 1937. However, it was not until 1940 that she was renamed *Monte Jata*, as photographed by a Giibraltar-based aircraft on 25th May 1944.

Aznar sold the veteran in 1953, but she continued giving service to other Spanish owners, first as *Corisco* and from 1961as *Socogui*. When broken up at Castellon in 1973, she had reached the venerable age of 64.

SENIOR SWEDES

As part of our tour of Europe's elderly tonnage, we visit Sweden in this issue, with photographs from the collections of Captain Hubert Hall and the editors. Captions have been based on career and other details in William Schell's *Registers*. Ships appear in order of building date.

FALKEN (above)
Craig, Taylor and Co., Stockton-on-Tees; 1893, 1,335gt, 237 feet
T. 3-cyl. by North Eastern Marine Engineering Co. Ltd., Sunderland
This photograph was taken on 2nd August 1945, as 500 tons of Polish coal is brought into Malmo by *Falken*, owned by Rederi A/B Falken (N.M. Thore) of Helsingborg. The ship was by then over fifty years old, and since 1934 had reverted to the name for which she had been built on the Tees, having been *Orion* between 1930 and 1934. Despite her age, in 1946 the veteran found a new owner who renamed her *Lungö*. She was broken up at Ystad in 1954 by A/B Carl Persson & Söner. Note the crate-like structure on deck: was this part of her life-saving apparatus? *Falken* also has doors in the bulwarks alongside her hatches possibly for carrying livestock. *[Otto Ohm, Malmo; Hubert Hall collection]*

BANANA (right)
Lobnitz and Co., Ltd., Renfrew; 1899, 1,273gt, 229 feet
T. 3-cyl. by Lobnitz and Co., Ltd., Renfrew
Given Sven Salen's domination of the reefer trade until their spectacular crash, and this ship's name, it is tempting to believe *Banana* was one of their earlier refrigerator ships, but evidence is against it. She was built as *Beira* for the DFDS service from the Baltic to the western Mediterranean, and the major published work on this Danish company mentions no refrigerated capacity. Further, she was given the name *Banana*, not by Salen but by a short-lived owner, Hans Elliot, who put her under the Panama flag in May 1939, Salen purchasing her in September 1939. It seems Salen was then more involved in the timber trade from the Baltic to the UK, and *Banana* probably entered this trade after the Second World War.

Builders Lobnitz were better known for dredgers and other specialised craft: see *Record* 26. Photographs show that, since completion as *Beira* (which ran for other Danish owners as *Ryaa* from 1937 to 1939) she had her top masts shortened and the wheelhouse enclosed. *Banana* was broken up at Bruges by Van Heyghen Frères in August 1951. *[Hubert Hall collection]*

BRITA (opposite top)
Sunderland Shipbuilding. Co., Ltd., Sunderland; 1908, 1,244gt, 231 feet
T. 3-cyl. by North Eastern Marine Engineering Co. Ltd., Sunderland
Seeming to stagger beneath the weight of her timber deck cargo, *Brita* steams into Preston some time in the late 1930s. Built as *Odland* for Norwegians, she had already had seven owners and also carried the named *Odland I* by 1928 when she moved to Sweden as *Brita*. The Maltese cross on the funnel dates this photograph after 1936, in which year *Brita* was

acquired by Fänges & Påhlssons Rederier. She had the misfortune to be detained by German occupation forces at Bergen on 9th April 1940 when on a seemingly innocent voyage from Uddevalla to Rouen with wood pulp. Presumably the destination of the cargo was sufficient to have her condemned by a prize court, and she was never to return to Swedish ownership. Under German control she was renamed *Desiderius Siedler*, but at war's end she was taken by the British as *Empire Connell*, notwithstanding Sweden's claim on her. The British Ministry of Transport then sold her to H.P. Lenaghan of Belfast, who registered her as *Ballyholme Bay* in the ownership of Irish Bay Lines Ltd., a company which owned a succession of interesting, if often semi-derelict craft (any further information on this owner would be welcomed). Life had one more change for the ship; in 1950 she moved to Hong Kong ownership as *Laurie Pattison*, and made it out to the Orient, being broken up in Hong Kong in 1952. *[J. and M. Clarkson]*

VINDÖ (below)
William Doxford and Sons, Ltd., Sunderland; 1909, 2,294gt, 290 feet
T. 3-cyl. by William Doxford and Sons, Ltd., Sunderland

It is not surprising that *Vindö* is looking drab and uncared for, as the turret ship is approaching the end of a long career, which was spent entirely under Scandinavian ownership. She was built for A. Broström & Son, Göteborg as *Inland*, becoming *Särimner* in 1934. For three years from 1939 she carried the same name under Finnish ownership, but was returned to Sweden in 1942 as *Ulla*. She was acquired by Rederi A/B Rex (K. M. Källström, manager) later that year, and ran as *Vindö* until 1958 when she became yet another ship to be broken up at Ystad by Carl Persson & Söner A/B. *[Hubert Hall collection]*

WINDAR (right, top)
Fredriksstad Mek. Verks., Fredrikstad, Norway; 1911, 1,136gt, 228 feet
T. 3-cyl. by Fredrikstad Mek. Verks., Fredrikstad
Although Norway in 1911 was not a notable shipbuilding nation, her builders did pioneer a type of vessel specially designed for the Scandinavian timber trade. The 'Fredrikstad' type had its masts clear of the holds to accommodate a full deck cargo. Built as *Figaro* for Norwegian owners, the *Windar* owned by Rederi A/B Norrström (I. Jeansson, manager) leaves the River Humber on 19th July 1956, after delivering a cargo of timber. She was near the end of her career: on 27th November 1956 *Windar* stranded in Kalmar Sound whilst sailing from London to Hurku with a cargo of coke. Although subsequently refloated, she was broken up at Ystad by A/B Carl Persson & Söner. *[D.H. Johnzon; Hubert Hall collection]*

KALIX (right, middle)
Sir Raylton Dixon & Co., Ltd., Middlesbrough; 1912, 2,734gt, 310 feet
T. 3-cyl. by North Eastern Marine Engineering Co. Ltd., Sunderland
Seen on trials, *Kalix* was built for the Swedish ore trade. Her original Stockholm owners, Rederi A/B Luleå-Ofoten (note the 'L O' on her funnel), becoming part of the better-known Trafik A/B Grängesberg-Oxelösund in 1916. *Kalix* then had a long and apparently uneventful career, being broken up at Ystad 1959 by A/B Carl Persson & Söner. *[Hubert Hall collection]*

OSMAN (opposite bottom)
Kockums Mek. Verks. A/B, Malmö; 1913, 1,316gt, 237 feet.
T. 3-cyl. by Kockums Mek. Verks. A/B, Malmö
Osman of C. W. Winck, Helsingborg shares a dry dock at Malmo with another of the owner's fleet, her sister *Oswin* (1,311/1913). Presumably the occasion which merited the flying of flags was their drydocking on their sale to Winck in 1921. *Osman* had been built as *Avesta* and *Oswin* as *Thai*, both for Rederi A/B Nordstjernan (A. A. Johnson), Stockholm.

Compared to the long-lived Swedish steamers featured here, *Osman* had a relatively brief 27-year life. She stranded and sank outside Risør on 16th March 1940 whilst carrying wood and general cargo from Göteborg to Hull. *[Otto Ohm, Malmo; Hubert Hall collection]*

NORDIC and **RÅDMANSÖ** (this page)
J. L. Thompson & Sons, Ltd., Sunderland; 1914, 4,182gt, 385 feet
T. 3-cyl. by Blair and Co. Ltd., Stocton-on-Tees

First of several examples of ships moving from liner to tramp trades is the *Nordic*, seen above in the ownership of Rederi A/B Transatlantic, Göteborg at Cape Town. In the lower photograph as Källström's *Rådmansö* - an identity she assumed in 1938 - she has been modified slightly for tramping. Gone are the frameworks for awnings, but she has gained temporary supports for what is presumably to be a coke cargo.
As were so many Swedish ships, in 1958 she was broken up at Ystad 1958 by Carl Persson & Söner A/B. *[Ships in Focus; Hubert Hall collection]*

MALMEN and **LJUSTERÖ**
N.V. Scheeps. Dordrecht, Dordrecht; 1919, 4,449gt, 352 feet
T. 3-cyl. by Maats. Fyenoord, Rotterdam
Within months, the young *Malmen* had three owners or managers. Launched for Rederi A/B Orient (B. M. Banck) of Stockholm, by the time of her delivery Rederi A/B Transatlantic of Göteborg had become managers. In 1920, *Malmen* was transferred to Rederi A/B Transatlantic, Göteborg, as seen in the above photograph. The lower shows her as *Ljusterö* after coming down in the world in 1936, working in the timber trade for the Källström family-managed Rederi A/B Rex of Stockholm. Judging by the rather unusual tug, the setting is a Swedish timber port, during or just after the Second World War. *Ljusterö* was broken up by A/B Carl Persson & Söner at Ystad in 1960. *[Ships in Focus and Hubert Hall collection]*

C.A. FALKLAND (above)
A/S Burmeister & Wain, Copenhagen; 1921, 7,032gt, 425 feet
12-cyl. 4SCSA oil engines by A/S Burmeister & Wain, Copenhagen
A feature on Swedish ships would not be complete without one of the motor ships that Scandinavia played such a large part in pioneering. The Danes were the leaders, but Swedish owners were not far behind, and this example was built as *Formosa* for A/B Svenska Ostasiatiska Kompaniet, Göteborg, albeit by the Danish yard that had built some of the first ocean-going motor ships. In 1953 the original owner renamed her *Kinaland*, but one year later she had assumed the identity seen here, *C.A. Falkland* managed by Axel Falkland of Helsingborg; the letter W on the funnel being explained by the name of the owning company, Rederi A/B Wallen. *C.A. Falkland* was broken up at Hong Kong in 1959 by Patt, Manfield and Co. *[Roy Fenton collection]*

ALFA (below)
P.Ph. Stuhrs Maskin & Skibsbyg. A/S, Aalborg; 1922, 1,257gt, 239 feet
T. 3-cyl. by A/S Frichs, Aarhus
It is noteworthy that Danish yards which were turning out motor ships like *C.A. Falkland* were contemporarily building traditional looking vessels like this, with a largely open bridge. Her original name *Senta* lasted just one year before she was sold from Denmark to Sweden to become *Kalmarsund XI*. Oscar A. Börjesson of Helsingborg acquired her in 1929 and gave her the name *Alfa*, which was painted, in an interesting little idiosyncracy which identifies his vessels, in a patriotic yellow with blue shading. After the war, *Alfa* was sold to further Swedish owners and became *Hollandia*. In 1957 she was put under the Panama flag by her last owner, Jean Courpas of Marseilles, who renamed her *Julia C*. Perhaps she became too old even for Panamanian registry, as in 1960 Courpas transferred her to the then fashionable Lebanese flag as *Aladdin*. She was broken up at La Spezia in 1963. *[J. and M. Clarkson]*

FREDEN
A/S Moss Værft, Moss; 1924, 1,191gt, 227 feet
T. 3-cyl. by A/S Moss Værft, Moss
A very full cargo of coke is restrained by wire netting and wooden stakes on the deck of *Freden*. The location is presumably a South Wales coal port, as behind her is just visible the electricity collier *John Hopkinson*.

Freden was built in Norway for Norwegian owners, moving without change of name to Sweden in 1929 when she was bought by Rederi A/B Ferlef, Stockholm. The 'S' initial of manager Anders Smith can just be seen on the funnel. Despite her 30 years, *Freden* found a further owner in 1954, and as the Hamburg-registered *Ingeborg* steamed on until broken up at Lübeck in 1960. *[G.E.P. Brownell]*

MAGNA
Fredriksstad Mek. Verks., Fredrikstad; 1929, 1,780gt, 269 feet
T-3-cyl. by Fredriksstad Mek. Verks., Fredrikstad
The ships of A/B Transmarin, Helsingborg became very familiar in UK west coast ports in post-war years. Photographed in a scenic setting, somewhere in Scandinavia, the *Magna* was built for the company, and her long bridge-deck design contrasts with the same builder's *Windar*.

In 1960 the ship was sold to Stockholm owners who put her under the Panama flag as *Soela*. She ended her days with Greek owners as *Ioulia*, abandoned after fire broke out in her engine room in the Gulf of Suez on 6th April 1969. She drifted aground about 75 miles south of Suez, and became a total loss. *[Roy Fenton collection]*

NAGARA (top and middle) and **DAGMAR** (bottom)
A/B Götaverken, Göteborg; 1929, 7,514gt, 437 feet
Oil engine 12-cyl. 4SCSA by A/B Götaverken, Göteborg
Despite being a motor ship, *Nagara* has considerable grace with her tall funnel, and it is not surprising that she originated with a liner company, A/B Svenska Ostasiatiska Kompaniet, for whom she served from 1929 to 1961.

When photographed as *Dagmar* in the early 1960s she was owned by a single-ship company managed by Tage Berglund of Göteborg. However, she still displays the funnel colours of her previous owner, Rederi A/B Timex also of Göteborg, for whom she ran very briefly as *Broriver*. Sale by Berglund in 1965 saw her become the Panama-flag *Ricardo* and in 1966 the *Bali Mariner* as which she was broken up at Kaohsiung in 1967. *[Hubert Hall collection (2); G.E.P. Brownell]*

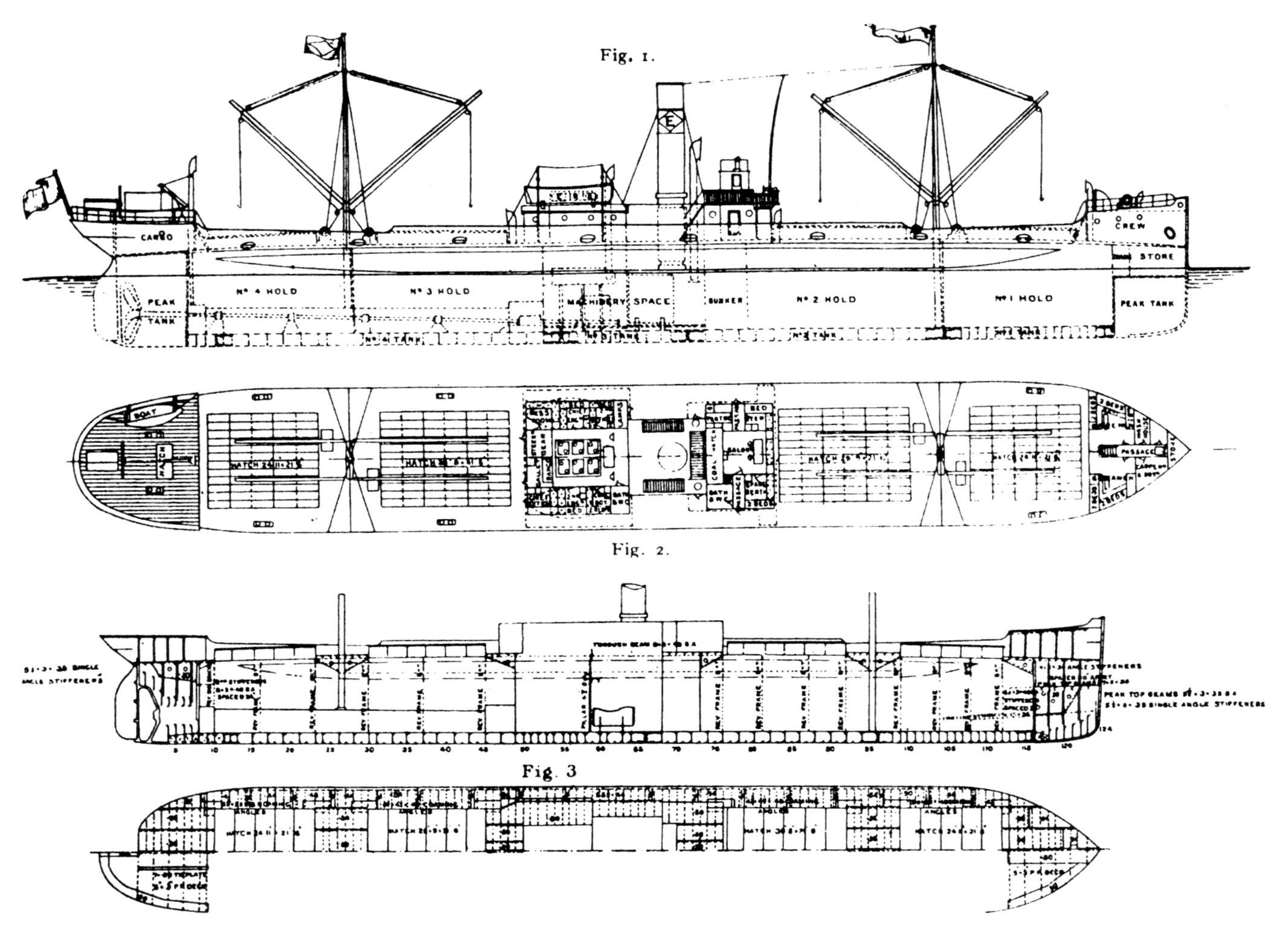

Above: General arrangement drawing of the first arch decker *Edenor*. Below: A drawing representing the midship's section of an arch deck vessel. Note how, beyond the hatch opening, the arch brackets and the deck beams almost give a continuous curve.

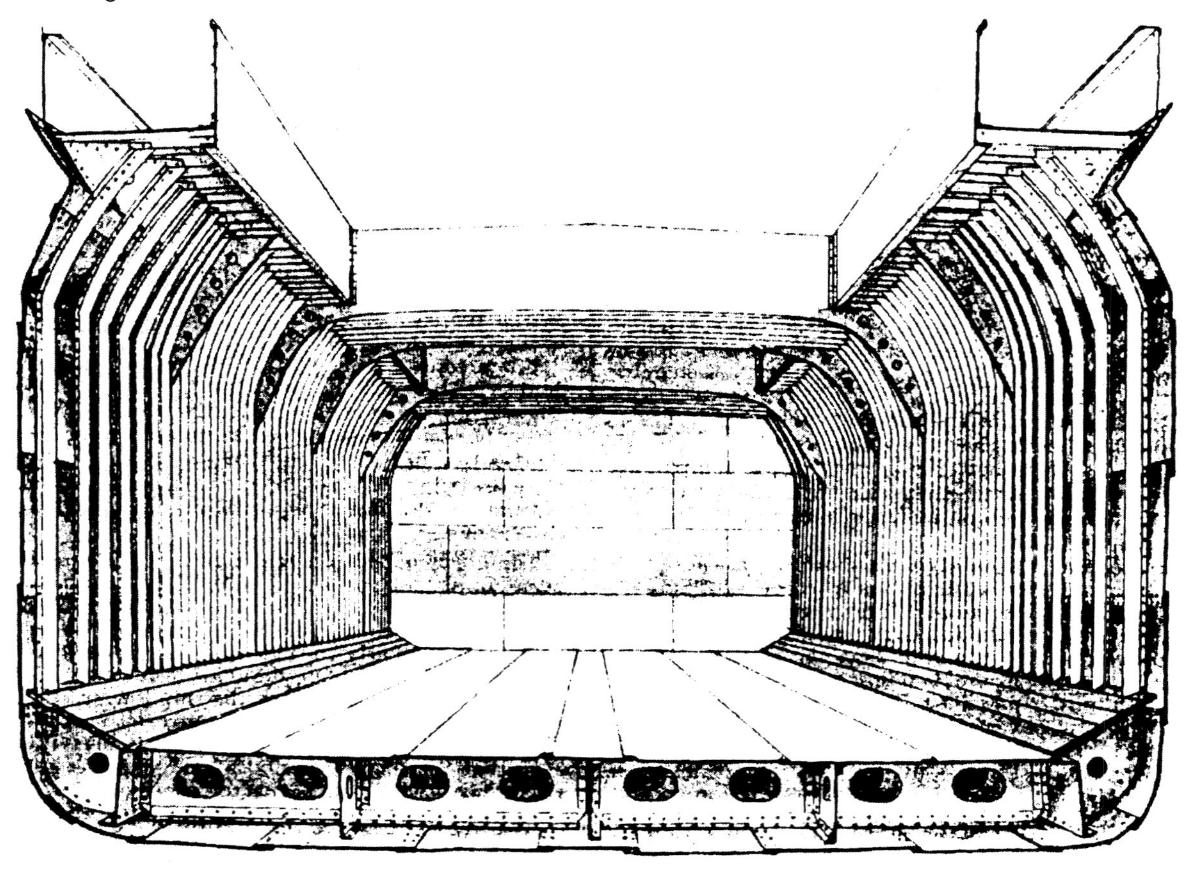

THE ARCH DECK STEAMERS

The Archers

Tramp shipping being a desperately competitive business, owners and - especially - builders of steamers intended for the tramp trades were continually searching for ways to make them cheaper to build or operate. The Doxford turret and Ropner's trunk-deck steamers are the most numerous and best known results of this quest, both offering ways to reduce operating costs by exploiting loopholes in regulations setting harbour and canal dues. A more radical approach was that adopted by the inventors of the Ayre-Ballard arch deck design, which gave a significant reduction in the quantity of steel needed for the hull, decreasing first cost. This feature is an attempt to explain the principles involved and catalogue the ships built to this design.

The principle

The major characteristic of the arch deck vessel was that the upper part of the hull was radiused inwards. The frames terminated at the point where the deck would be placed in a conventional ship, and were joined to the deck beams by arched brackets. Stringers joined the arch brackets along the length of the ship, the combination acting like a girder and giving good longitudinal strength.

The designer took advantage of the extra freeboard which the arch deck design gave to adopt another novel feature: reverse sheer. This was a sound engineering principle, as the inverse sheer supported the weight of cargo, engines and deck erections better than in a ship with normal sheer. It was possible to adopt reverse sheer and maintain the vessel's sea-keeping qualities because the ship was some seven feet higher amidships than a conventional vessel of the same size. This meant the height of the forecastle and poop above the water was equivalent to that of a conventional vessel. The reverse sheer was not a necessary feature of the arch deck design, and at least two of the later ships had straight-line sheer. The first two completed, *Edenor* and *Sheaf Arrow*, certainly had the reverse sheer, and appear broken backed

A writer in the 'Marine Engineer and Naval Architect' in January 1913 maintained that the vessels had proven to be dry boats and very comfortable. 'The sloping sides takes the venom out of the waves', he wrote, 'so that their effect on rolling is much reduced.' He continued that the arched sides also threw the waves back on themselves, leaving the deck relatively dry. Ballard himself wrote in 1923 that '...invariably excellent reports had been received of their weatherly qualities. Reduced pitching and scending has been substantiated in a most marked fashion, and this, with the absence of wells to fill in heavy weather, enables the Arch vessel to maintain better speed and passage times than ships of the ordinary type.'

The arch effectively extended the capacity of the hold upwards, and this allowed a greater cubic capacity than a conventional ship, and much better reserve buoyancy: 33% more according to Ballard's calculations on the *Edenor*.

The combination of the arch and the reverse sheer gave the hull structure high integral strength. In a paper published in 'The Shipbuilder' in 1913, Ballard includes calculations which show that the stresses on a conventional hull were greater than on the arch deck hull in hogging condition (i.e. when the midsection of the hull, and not the extremities, are supported by water).

The strength of the arch decker's hull allowed a saving in the amount of steel needed. Ballard maintained that the reduction was 18% and, even allowing for modest exaggeration on his part, this saving was significant. Ballard claimed for the first arch decker, *Edenor*, that 'The steel used was the lightest weight for a given deadweight and speed ever attained', and that 'This vessel was the cheapest steel sea-going vessel, to full classification, ever to have been built and probably will remain so.' Writing in 1921, when experience had been gained, Ballard made a more modest claim, quoting the saving in steelwork as between 10 and 14% compared with a conventional vessel of the same dimensions.

Although Ballard claimed that arch deckers had also been used to carry grain, timber and pitprops, the design was particularly suitable for colliers. The lack of a need for pillars gave a clear hold for easier discharge and the inward sloping sides made the ships self-trimmers.

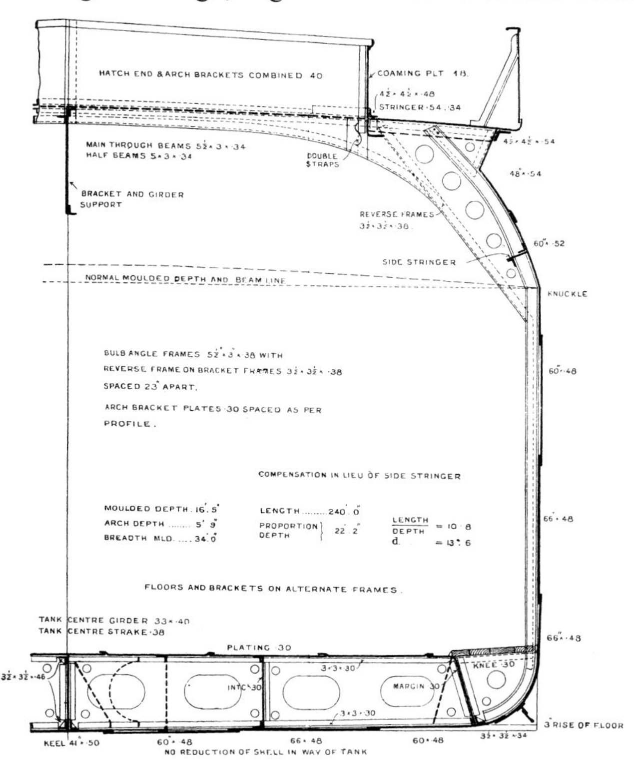

A midships section of *Edenor*.

Above: *Edenor,* the first arch deck vessel completed. *[J.& M.Clarkson collection]*
Below: Souter's *Sheaf Arrow* in the Avon, showing the arch deck construction. She was described as 'the fastest collier on the north-east coast', in a 1913 technical paper. *[J. and M. Clarkson]*

The designers
The arch deck design is credited to Maxwell Ballard. After an apprenticeship with Robert Stephenson and Co. Ltd. at Hebburn, he was employed by Workman, Clark and Co. Ltd. at Belfast, returning to the Tyne in 1909 to work on the arch deck design in collaboration with one of the Ayre brothers. This was probably Wilfred, who at the time was working for Wood, Skinner and Co. Ltd. at Bill Quay. Ayre did not continue with the project and it was Ballard who took out the patent, but the design is generally referred to as the Ayre-Ballard arch deck type. Swan, Hunter and Wigham Richardson also became involved, possibly obtaining rights to the patent from Ballard, and their subsidiaries built some of earlier examples of the design. The connection with the Ayres continued: the brothers' own yard at Burntisland built three arch deck ships after the First World War.

The outcome
The order for the first arch deck ship *Edenor*, was won in 1909, but thanks to an industrial dispute involving the lock-out of boilermakers, she was not delivered until 1911. The second arch decker, *Sheaf Arrow*, went to W.A. Souter of Newcastle-upon-Tyne, an owner who was eventually to have the largest fleet of these ships, numbering seven.

The first arch decker from the Londonderry yard of the North of Ireland Shipbuilding Co. Ltd., a Swan, Hunter subsidiary, was built as a speculation and launched with the name *Pennyburn* after a district of Londonderry. The four-month gap between the launch of this builder's second vessel and its being registered as *Glenfoyle* suggests that she too was built without a definite buyer. These two engines-aft ships went to work on the Canadian canals, along with *Thyra Menier* and *Honoreva*, two engines amidships arch deckers built in England for a Bristol company which had Canadian connections.

Furness Withy took two of the type, *Pensacola* and *Bedale*, for comparison with conventional ships and another design which was being offered at the time, the Monitor type. The company bought the Monitor *Wingate* and chartered two others, *Monitoria* and *Hyltonia*. By the time building of the arch deck type paused in 1917, a total of 14 had been completed, mostly for collier owners. The type was evidently best suited for carrying coal: the *Edenor*, initially used in the Baltic trade, returned to the east coast coal trade in 1915.

In 1921 the design reappeared, with a renewed campaign by Ballard in the technical press to arouse interest, and there was a flurry of orders, some 13 further ships being completed. As well as the three from Burntisland, most of the balance came from Blyth, with the final example, as late as 1928, from Swan, Hunter.

Ballard, in a letter to 'Sea Breezes' in April 1953, claimed that the building of many more ships to the arch deck design was prevented only by the outbreak of the Second World War, which also stopped the Japanese building the design under license. However, this claim must be doubted as the last recorded example is the *Sac 6*, completed in 1928. If interest in the design had continued, Burntisland and other yards would surely have built further examples as the momentum of shipbuilding grew in the years immediately before the Second World War.

The reckoning
If Ballard's claim was correct that the arch deck vessels were stronger than contemporary shelter deck vessels, they would be expected to have survived better. Does their record bear this out? Leaving aside the heavy wartime losses - no fewer than eight in the First and nine in the Second World War - only five arch deck vessels survived to be scrapped, whilst five were wrecked or foundered. Of those that went to the breakers, the youngest was *Sheaf Arrow* at a mere 22

One of the longest lived arch deck ships, and the one to have carried the most names, seen here with her last, *Irene M.* *[World Ship Society Photo Library]*

This page top: *Sheaf Don* is coaling the German battleship *Friedrich der Grosse*, presumably when the latter was in Allied hands after the First World War. *[Kevin O'Donoghue collection]*

Middle: *Danapris. [J. & M.Clarkson collection]*

Bottom: *Sheaf Crest* in Gallions Reach, River Thames on 24th July 1937. *[R. A. Snook, Kevin O'Donoghue collection]*

Opposite top: Carlbeath in a Mediterranean port, probably having discharged a coal cargo. *[Kevin O'Donoghue collection]*

Opposite bottom: Photographed in J.B. Marshall's ownership, *Ayton* was destined to be the last survivor of the arch deck vessels, although her last three years were spent as a wreck in Piraeus harbour. *[Roy Fenton collection]*

years, albeit at the depths of a depression, whilst the oldest was the original vessel, which survived 48 years. The average is almost 40 years. Of the five which became peacetime casualties, only one was certainly due to stress of weather, the 11-year old *Sheaf Brook* which disappeared in a North Sea storm during November 1935. In both longevity and ability to stand up to bad weather, the arch deck ships had a good record, which appears to support their designer's claim of additional strength.

So why was a strong, cheap and apparently well-proven design not perpetuated beyond 27 examples? The most likely reason was the steady decline of British coal exports following the First World War, and particularly after the industrial unrest of the late 1920s. The arch deck design seems to have appealed largely to owners with relatively small steamers running in the medium-distance coal trades, with the largest built being a modest 320 feet in length, and with a gross tonnage under 3,000. Whilst larger tramps continued to be built when shipping recovered from the depression, the coal trade needed fewer of the smaller ships of the size represented by the arch deckers. The design had found a niche market amongst owners of medium-sized collier, but the failure to demonstrate that larger arch deck vessels could be economical and safe led to its extinction when the need for the smaller colliers declined. The arch deck design was successful, in construction and operating if not aesthetic terms, but was sadly short lived.

A loose end

A loose end remains to be tied up: the actual number of arch deck ships built. In his 'Sea Breezes' letter, Ballard mentions 'some 28' arch deck vessels being built. Only 27 can be positively identified, and one is left wondering how accurate was Ballard's memory. For instance, he quotes the *Edenor* as being sunk by a U-boat in 1943, when in fact she survived to be broken up in 1959. It could be that he was counting as two ships the *Thirlmere* which was renamed *Eskmere* between launch and completion.

[To be continued]

THE LAST SQUARE RIGGERS BUILT FOR BRITISH OWNERS

John Naylon

In his article 'More days more dollars – two testing voyages' (*Record* 26) Tony Westmore reminded us of the unpredictable nature of sailing-ship performances, a factor contributing to the commercial windjammer's inevitable demise. He also remarked of the *Archibald Russell* (1905) that she is 'popularly thought of as being the last square rigger to be built for British owners', rightly implying that this is not the case.

Basil Lubbock may have started this hare running. In *The Last of the Windjammers*, Vol.II, page 126, he states 'Hardie's *Archibald Russell* was the last big square rigger launched from a British yard for general cargo trade' (although by page 307 of the same work he is trimming somewhat: 'This four-mast barque ... was one of the last square-rigged sailing ships to be built on the Clyde'). The belief has been perpetuated by other authorities. Thus, Harold Underhill in *Deep-Water Sail*, p.223, declares that J. Hardie & Co. '... when instructing Scotts of Greenock to build *Archibald Russell* ... were in fact giving what proved to be the last order ever placed by a British ship-owner for sailing ship tonnage ...'. And no doubt credence was lent to the story by the publicity given to the *Russell* while she was under Erikson's ownership in the interwar grain races and by her survival until 1949.

Neither the *Sunlight* (opposite) nor the *Rendova* (above) was particularly squarely rigged (as most bald-headers were, to compensate for the absence of royals) and their scanty sail plan is apparent – no doubt accounting for their reputations as poor sailers. Strangely, although lower and topmasts were in one on fore and main, the mizzen had a fidded topmast. *[Both: State Library of Victoria, opposite: H99.220/1186, above: H99.220/3250]*

Sunlight and *Rendova*

Although the *Archibald Russell* tradition is so embedded that it is still being repeated in serious maritime publications, in fact the last two commercial square riggers built in a British yard for British owners were the *Sunlight* and *Rendova*, completed in 1907 for Lever Brothers of Port Sunlight, Cheshire, and registered in Liverpool with official numbers 124033 and 124046.

Three-masted steel barques of 1,432 gross and 1,315 net tons, the sister ships were launched on the Clyde in January (*Sunlight*) and February (*Rendova*) 1907 by Napier & Miller Ltd. of Old Kilpatrick, Dunbartonshire, with yard numbers 155 and 156. Their dimensions were virtually identical: 230.9 x 37.2 x 21.0 feet in the case of the *Sunlight*, with a 38-foot poop and a 33-foot forecastle. The *Rendova* measured 231.1 feet, her poop was three feet shorter, and her under-deck tonnage was 1,295 compared with the 1,298 of the *Sunlight*. Their signal letters were HKDN (*Sunlight*) and HKLV (*Rendova*).

Lever Brothers' choice of builder was curious, given the wealth of experience of sailing-ship construction on the Clyde. For most of their existence Napier & Miller had only built steamers. Similarly, Lever Brothers' venture into deep-sea ship-owning was odd. Although they operated fleets of very small steamers and barges to service their factories and depots at Port Sunlight and Sydney, N.S.W., none of the directors knew much of the details of ship management and they therefore had to engage an outside firm to manage the *Sunlight* and *Rendova*: John McDowell, with offices in Port Sunlight.

Bulk oil tankers

The barques belonged to that rare species of sailing vessel – the bulk oil tanker. The lower hold was subdivided by nine bulkheads. A large donkey engine forward of the poop served the tanks with powerful pumps, and the tanks had steam coils in the bottom to reduce the consistency of the oil should it become too thick for pumping. Tanks and 'tween decks could be used for other cargoes or for a mix of bulk oil and dry cargo.

In other respects, too, they were functional-looking departures from the orthodox, unlike the handsome and conventionally-designed *Archibald Russell*. They were stump-topgallant or jubilee rigged (carrying no royals); the steel decks were unsheathed; the stockless anchors, stowed in the hawse pipes, were hove up by a messenger from a steam winch on the main deck. There was no deckhouse, so that the crew presumably berthed in the actual forecastle – a real throwback.

The *Sunlight* and *Rendova* were conceived as bringing palm oil from Rendova Island in the Pacific to Port Sunlight for soap manufacture. In practice, they usually went out to the oil mills of Levers' Pacific Plantations Ltd., of Sydney, N.S.W., and as time went by engaged in other trades as well. For example, during a 30-month absence from the Mersey, the *Rendova*, besides bringing coconut oil from Sydney, picked up petroleum in New York (three times) and Philadelphia (once) and delivered it to the Spanish ports of Sevilla (three times), Alicante, La Coruña and Gijón. In 1910 the *Sunlight* was chartered by the United Molasses Company and in 1914 was loading bulk molasses and bagged sugar in Haiti.

The barques could be economically manned with 17-20 crew but were reckoned to be poor sailers, heavy to manoeuvre and constantly broaching-to when running in bad weather. The *Rendova* came on to the reinsurance market on her maiden passage to Australia.

In this rare photograph, kindly provided by Dr. Jürgen Meyer and taken from U 59 shortly before she sank the barque, the *Snespurven* ex-*Rendova* is clearly displaying her neutral markings. Curiously, most of the barque's sails have been given a harbour stow, suggesting that when intercepted she was proceeding under lower staysails, headsails and the goose-winged fore lower topsail, and was near port, expecting a tow or an escort. *[Dr.J.Meyer collection]*

War losses

Both vessels were sunk by German submarines during the First World War, in the dangerous southern approaches to the Irish Sea. The *Sunlight* was the first to go, in 1915. As reported in Lever Brothers' house magazine: 'The German submarine fired three shots across the bows of our sailing ship, then came under the stern to read the name and port of registry, and afterwards, without any inquiry, signalled Captain Dagwell to abandon ship. All hands, twenty in number, left the ship in two boats, and the barque was torpedoed. This occurred at 4 p.m. on Sunday, June 6th 20 miles south-west of Galley Head, i.e., between Cape Clear and Kinsale. The crew were in the boats, pulling towards land, for twelve hours; then were fortunately rescued by a government trawler, *Indian Empire*, and brought into Queenstown.'

The *Rendova*, which in 1915 had been sold to Vestlandske Petroleums Kompagni of Bergen, Norway (perhaps as a consequence of the loss of the *Sunlight*), and renamed *Snespurven*, was a victim of Germany's declaration, in February 1917, of unrestricted U-boat warfare. Neutral ships were to be regarded as enemy ships if found between the Bay of Biscay and the Faeroes, and during March and April 1917 the average number of neutral Norwegian vessels sunk was more than two per day. The *Snespurven* (Captain E. Brumqvist) was caught on 2 April 1917 in the St.George's Channel by U 59, commanded by Freiherr von Fircks, while on passage New York to Dublin with petroleum, and was sunk by gunfire.

FROM THE BOSUN'S LOCKER

John Clarkson

Over the first twenty eight issues of *Record* your editors have had no problem finding sufficient material for each issue. To the contrary, and as our contributors well know, articles have often to wait for suitable slots where their content will fit in well with others in the same issue. What has been neglected are the 'bits and pieces', often put to one side to fill the odd half page which rarely materialises.

What do these 'bits and pieces' consist of one might ask. There are numerous items which could find their way into *Record* through these pages. It is not easy to list all, in fact there is no list and we are open to offers of suitable material. There could be news items, relating to ships and shipping, but not the sort of news which appears in the shipping magazines available on the magazine shelves and often repeated in all three. News about people, places, photograph collections, shipping related exhibitions etc. Our readers can help by submitting useful possible items.

On the subject of people there is one thing none of us can escape and all too often our passing is not recorded. The well known usually get mentioned but in the short lifetime of *Record* a number of good friends have passed away without notice. We feel they deserve mention and this will be corrected for three dedicated researchers in this issue.

Photographic matters are another subject and perhaps the one which will take up most space. This can cover a multitude of facets, ships in strange places or situations, ships to be identified, but please not the ship photographed at a distance of three miles on a wet day whilst on holiday in Blackpool three years ago.

Under this heading we could include ships in port – in ports which no longer exist or in places we would like identified. The column may be used to appeal for help. We have our regular sources for illustrations but sometimes admit defeat only to be told by a reader after publication 'if only you had asked me.....' At the present time some publishers are tending to be more secretive for commercial reasons but through openness and trust we believe we can provide better and more complete publications.

A subject which we have almost kept completely clear of has been book reviews. There are books which deserve praise and there are others about which 'least said, soonest mended' applies. There are also occasionally books from the past which we see and which deserve a little write up. They may no longer be available but you can always keep an eye open for them in the second-hand dealers' lists.

These are just a few ideas about what may be covered. Your editors hope that you will find *From the Bosun's Locker* to be interesting, lively and containing material which hasn't appeared elsewhere. At the same time we may win a few more subscribers and, you never know, it may be your way of getting into *Record*.

We haven't any news as such to report in *Record 29* but what we do have are some photographs which are unidentified but interesting. We will give what we know about the pictures prefixed by a short reference number. Should you write to us about any of the photos please quote this number to avoid any doubt as to which picture your comments refer.

Good reading and do let us know of anything suitable for inclusion.

OBITUARIES

Peter Kenyon, a lifelong friend, passed away in January at the age of seventy eight. I first came into contact with Peter when I joined the World Ship Society way back in 1958. In those days new members' names and addresses were passed to local branch secretaries and Peter, then secretary of the Preston Branch and always keen, got on his bike and rode over from Leyland to Longton, about 5 or 6 miles, to make contact.

Born in Deepdale, Preston not far from Preston North End's ground, Peter was a plumber by trade. His entire working life except for his period of national service was in the massive Royal Ordinance Factory at Euxton. He served his national service in the Fleet Air Arm and even then never went to sea.

In the early 1960s, by which time Peter had a car, we made a few trips to Hull for a day's photography. Steam trawlers were still plentiful and Victoria Dock, used for timber imports, was still in full swing with timber everywhere. No motorways, we left at about 4am and got back about 10pm. As a tribute to Peter the pictures from one of our days out will become an article in a future *Record*.

Over the years we kept in touch. For a period after retiring he was part of a team cleaning and identifying negatives from the Stewart Bale Collection at the Maritime Museum in Liverpool. By the late nineties Peter was tiring of travelling to Liverpool and became a regular visitor to Longton, helping with various matters relating to *Ships in Focus* publications, photographs and our negative collection. Sometimes filing prints but mainly researching negatives, he was always happy with a pile of negatives and a *Lloyds Register*. His other great interest, besides his family, was preserved steam railways but he always came back to shipping and in particular Preston shipping. Over many years he built up registers of Preston arrivals and sailings along with details and photos of many of the ships.

Peter would have been in his glory with the British part of Alex Duncan's collection to catalogue and how we would have appreciated his endeavours. This was not to be. Peter went into hospital in mid January and died within days leaving behind his wife Doris and son Andrew. Two days later his first great grandchild was born, an event he had been greatly looking forward to.

Peter, thank you for all your help, advice and encouragement over the years.

Norman Taylor of Gosport died on 30th July 2003 at Poole in Dorset only one day short of being eighty six, leaving his wife Joan and two sons, Stephen and Albert. Norman was born at Eccles, Lancashire in 1917 and became interested in ships while visiting the nearby Manchester Ship Canal.

After leaving school he was apprenticed as a draughtsman and moved to Gosport in 1939 taking up a position with Vospers, remaining with them until retirement came in 1981. Being in a reserved occupation Norman was refused permission to join the armed forces in the Second World War but joined the Home Guard and also served as a fire watcher.

Norman was a renowned and award winning model maker in his day. One of his models was of the *San Demetrio* displayed at the Imperial War Museum. A request to become a professional model maker was turned down. He was interested in all merchant ships but particularly in British tramp steamers. An expert photographic printer and excelling at copying he was extremely good at identifying 'unknown' ships.

When the *Bristol Series* of glass plate negatives was split up he became custodian of the tramp steamers section and later, after the demise of Mr.W.Bryant, of the British and foreign coasters. He also probably had the largest holding of what survived of the Downs negatives taken on the Manchester Ship Canal. We corresponded many times on the subject of ship photographs and he was one of those people to whom we could always turn to for that elusive photograph.

Norman's health deteriorated over the last couple of years and sadly part of his photo collection was lost in a house fire. Much of the remainder was rendered useless by smoke damage. Luckily he had parted with most of his glass plates over the last year or two and those he had held on to appear to have survived being protected by the original cardboard boxes in which they were stored.

Thank you Norman for all you have contributed to illustrating maritime history and for your knowledge of British tramp shipping.

Ian Graham Stewart was not known personally by your editors and perhaps very few of our readers in the UK would have met or corresponded with him. What he was well known for were two books, *Liberty Ships in Peacetime* and *British Tramps*, both excellent, out of print for a number of years and much sought after. A third book not so well known in the UK was *The Ships that serve New Zealand – British & European Lines* published in 1964. In recent years Ian had worked on a book about Singapore shipping but it is unlikely this will now come to fruition.

Ian was born in Wanganui where his father Captain R. D. Stewart was Harbourmaster and later master of the *River City*. From his early days he had a love of the sea, was a good artist and wrote on matters maritime, in fact he wrote his first article at the age of twelve for an English shipping magazine. After school he worked for a couple of years with the Holm Shipping Company and then with the New Zealand Shipping Company throughout New Zealand, qualifying as a chartered shipbroker and marine insurance assessor. In 1961 he moved to Bluff and set up business as a cargo surveyor and marine insurance assessor. He was shipping correspondent for the *Southland Times* and wrote for magazines such as *N Z Marine News*. 1971 saw Ian moving first to Newcastle, Australia and then to Perth as an assessor for New Zealand Insurance and establishing his own assessing business. Whilst in Australia he produced his two most important books and became known as a world authority on shipping matters.

By 2002 Ian was in the early stages of Alzheimer's disease and went back to New Zealand to be near his sister, his wife and son having died and his daughters moved overseas. Ian passed away peacefully in May 2004. We all must quietly say thank you to him for the knowledge and research he has left behind in his books and articles.

To the families of Peter, Norman and Ian we send our deepest sympathies.

The Bristol Series

As mentioned above Norman Taylor held part of the *Bristol Series* of negatives. We know part of the collection – those of Scandinavian ships - went to a collector in Oslo and what could be described as local ships – small Bristol coasters, tugs and dredgers, plus all the sailing ships - went to Bristol Museum. Is there anyone out there who knows the history of the collection, who took the photos, what happened to him or her, who took custody of the collection and organised the split up? This could be an interesting story and lead to a few picture articles for *Record*. All leads and information will be greatly appreciated and acknowledged.

What ships are these

To conclude our first *From the Bosun's Locker* we have a selection of photographs where we hope you can identity the ship featured or the situation. What information we have we will give alongside the photo. As mentioned earlier, to avoid confusion please quote the reference number of the print in any replies.

01/29 There are no clues of any sort on the back of this photograph as to where or when it was taken.
The ship appears to be a smallish liner but the considerable bridge on her after end is unusual - so perhaps a ferry. Closer examination of the tug offers no clues except that her funnel is in a single colour with no bands or other markings apparent. The picture has been taken in a hot climate judging from the headwear of the people in the boat in the foreground.

02/29 A fine study of the old steam tug *Flying Foam*. But which *Flying Foam* and where was the photograph taken? Again there are no clues on the reverse. No signs of smoke or steam and only two men onboard, one holding on to the line on the after end could suggest she had been pushed off from the quay to pose for her photograph. The type of photograph, its colour and the mounting are appropriate for the late 1800s or early 1900s.

03/29 This photograph taken in Penzance harbour should not be too difficult to identify as we are sure someone will have a named copy of the print which was produced by Gibson & Sons, Scilly Isles. There is nothing to indicate what had befallen the ship or when.

SD14: THE SURVIVORS

SD14: The Full Story by John Lingwood is due to be published by Ships in Focus in December 2004. Interest in these ships is considerable, as they may be said to represent the last flowering of British shipbuilding and ship design. Rather than wait until the very last SD14 or Prinasa 121 had disappeared from the seas, it was decided to publish now, when a number still trade, even though that meant we could not write the last word on these ships. However, so that we can tell as full a story as possible, we intend from time to time to include updates in *Record* and lists of which ships are still believed to be trading.

For the list below we are indebted to Nigel Jones, who has drawn on data very kindly made available by David Hazell and Simon Smith who run The Shipping Information Service, which can be contacted by e-mail at shipinform@aol.com

In addition to those ships listed below, which are believed to be in service, Nigel has listed another 20 for which no movements have been reported for several years and some may have been broken up. These are not listed below, as details are included in *SD14: The Full Story*.

Yard No.	Name	Year	Flag	Location or selected ports 2003/4
Austin & Pickersgill, Southwick, Sunderland				
906	JIN DA HAI	1976	China	
1377	TANIA	1977	Georgia	Santa Cruz de Tenerife, Alexandria
1378	QING JIANG	1978	China	Busan, Rizhao
1380	SONG DUONG	1979	Vietnam	Jo Sichang , Manila
1381	PING JIANG	1978	China	Karachi, Djibouti
1383	AN YANG JIANG	1980	China	Ho Chi Minh City, Nampo
1384	THAI BINH	1980	Vietnam	Singapore, Mesaieed
1385	AN DONG JIANG	1979	China	Kuwait, Qatar
1387	EVER BRIGHT	1979	Panama	Singapore, Ko Sichang
1390	STURDY FALCON	1980	Vietnam	Cape Town, Santos
1391	PANGANI	1980	Singapore	Paradip, Port Klang
1394	SPRING	1979	Unknown	Pulau Batam
1396	RYONG GANG 2	1980	North Korea	Reunion, Durban
1397	SHUN YUAN 6	1980	Hong Kong	Kochi (India), Tanjung Pelepas
1400	SAIGON 3	1980	Vietnam	Santos, Cotonou
1401	SAIGON 5	1980	Vietnam	Conakry, Jubail
1403	HUN JIANG	1981	China	Hong Kong, Shanghai
1414	YUAN JIANG	1981	China	Mumbai , Macau
1415	FAR EAST	1982	Vietnam	Freetown, Pasir Gudang
1417	CHANG PING	1982	Singapore	Dalian, Dar es Salaam
1418	HYANG RO BONG	1982	North Korea	Batangas, Colombo
1426	ODELIS	1985	Panama	Havana (laid up)
Bartrams/Austin & Pickersgill, South Dock, Sunderland				
428	SHU DE	1971	China	Hong Kong
446	PAVONIS	1975	St. Vincent	Yangon, Chittagong
448	NAVAL GENT	1975	Panama	Luanda, Tartous
461	HERMES	1977	Thai	Kuwait, Colombo
464	NANKING	1978	Jordan	Umm Qasr, Gizan
Hellenic Shipyards, Skaramanga				
1063	SAM HAI 1	1970	North Korea	Maizuru
1064	LI JIA	1970	China	China
1073	SEA VENTURE	1972	U.S.A.	Philadelphia, Charleston
CCN, Rio de Janeiro (**Prinasa 121 derivatives of the SD14 design*)				
092	THETIS	1974	Unknown	Great Bitter Lakes (arrested)
123	LISA L	1979	Mongolia	Port Sudan, Ruwais
127	JING REN	1977	China	China
130	FORTUNE SEA	1979	Panama	Nanjing, Surabaya
132*	LONG FU	1980	Panama	Rizhao, Jo Sichang
134*	AMAR	1980	North Korea	Kakinada, Belawan
141	ORIENTAL KIKU	1983	Unknown	Lianyungang
143	NAMA	1988	Panama	Piraeus, Noukakchott
145	GASPARD	1981	Panama	Antwerp, East London
147	SAFMARINE EVAGELIA	1981	Malta	Cape Town, Durban
151	SAFMARINE MEROULA	1981	Cyprus	Walvis Bay, Matadi
152	JAIPUR	1981	Jordan	Jebel Ali, Mombasa
153	RA NAM	1982	North Korea	Kakinada, Qinzhou
155*	JAT NA MU	1982	Singapore	Chittagong, Kandla
156	ORIENTAL PEACE	1983	Panama	Abidjan, Gibraltar
157	SAFMARINE CONGO	1983	Cyprus	Durban, Onne
158	LONG XIANG	1983	Hong Kong	Haiphong, Hong Kong
159	MANASLU	1983	Cyprus	Taichung, Keelung
160	JORDAN II	1988	St. Vincent	Hodeidah, Massawa
Robb Caledon, Dundee				
D569	JA GANG	1977	North Korea	Penglai, Xingang
AFNE, Ensenada				
47	ADREKNI	1978	St. Vincent	Chennai, Bandar Imam Khomeini
Smith's Dock, South Bank, Middlesbrough				
1349	ALDONA	1983	Panama	Dakar, Havana
1350	LOTUS ISLANDS	1983	Panama	Santarem, Bizerta (to be r/n WENG)
1357	PHUONG DONG 03	1986	Vietnam	Bedi, Dakar
1358	PHUONG DONG 01	1986	Vietnam	Matanzas (Cuba), Tema
1359	PHUONG DONG 02	1986	Vietnam	Aden, Kandla

BLUE STAR'S THREE Cs

Captain A.W. Kinghorn

California Star at Wellington. *[Ian Farquhar collection]*

Following the completion of the highly successful 'Imperial Star' class of 12,000 ton, six-hatch cargo liners during the middle thirties ('Record' 9) the company decided to build three smaller ships for their developing West Coast of North America service. This ran from the UK, through the Panama Canal (having taken bunkers at Caracas Bay, Curacao) to Vancouver, New Westminster and ports south down to Los Angeles - a round voyage usually of some three and a half months.

A surge of shipbuilding which preceded the outbreak of war in 1939 meant that no British firm could promise early delivery, so for the first time a continental yard was selected: Burmeister and Wain of Copenhagen. The new ships were to be of approximately 8,300 gt, five-hatch, 12-passenger, mainly refrigerated vessels but also with ample space for non-reefer cargoes such as borax, dried fruit, cotton and timber - crated veneers as well as sawn planks. Outward cargoes would be general, British exports in all shapes and sizes.

The new design

They would follow the company's latest single-masted style which meant the 'foremast' white steaming navigation light had to be hoisted on the forestay - lowered in port when working cargo at number 1. It was often found at sea - especially on a dark, damp night - that the reflection of this light on the wet jackstaff truck was mistaken on the bridge for another ship's light dead ahead. There was no radar of course and not even a gyro compass, although their big immediate predecessors had Sperry gyros with auto steering built in. But the three new ships had electric steering suitable for conversion to auto steering if and when gyro compasses became available.

Gyro compasses, then, were all needed for the Royal Navy. The two big brass engine room telegraphs port and starboard stood dramatically on the wooden deck outside the varnished teak wheelhouse. They, and all the other outside brass, copper fittings and the brass trumpet whistle on the funnel, took a lot of polishing!

For the first time there was to be no cargo hatch between funnel and navigation bridge. Positioned at the forward end of the boat deck this latter was always considered (by her masters and deck officers) a deck too low, visibility ahead being largely obscured by the high forecastle head. To compensate for this a steering wheel on a brass spindle up from the wheelhouse enabled the ship to be steered and navigated from the monkey island, over which a canvas awning was rigged in the tropics. An array of highly polished copper voicepipes led to the deck below for transmitting engine room telegraph orders and a Perspex-covered dropdown chart table protected the chart in use from showers of rain.

Paint style was the by-then famous funnel, white superstructure, buff yellow masts and black hull with forecastle and poop overside in white, but lacking the

Above: *California Star. [Roy Fenton collection]*

Right and below: *Canadian Star* at Cape Town. *[J. & M. Clarkson collection]*

Opposite page: *Canadian Star* photographed by the Royal New Zealand Air Force off Gisborne 8th September 1941. *[Ian Farquhar collection]*

latter day white bulwarks or the white line which had moved up and down from boot top to sheerstrake since the company's early 'Brod-' ships carried it pre-First World War. Whereas the big two-funnelled South American liners' names all began with 'A' - *Arandora Star*, for example - these new ships would have 'C' names, conveniently suiting the trade. Yard number 639 was *California Star*, launched on 6th August 1938. Number 640 was *Canadian Star*, launched 20th October, while 641 *Columbia Star* came down the ways on 15th February 1939, completing during May - only four months before the outbreak of hostilities.

The three ships were as identical as such a trio could be, all powered by - as would be expected - the builder's own engines - six-cylinder diesels driving a single screw. Comfortable accommodation, including forward main lounge and an after smoking room, was provided for 12 first-class passengers. Captain, radio officer and fourth mate were accommodated abaft the navigation bridge at the forward end of the boat deck, with the passenger accommodation on the deck below. Officers' cabins, washrooms and messrooms were below on the main deck, with ratings and petty officers aft. Cooks' and stewards' accommodation was amidships below the main deck. Passenger accommodation was panelled in polished wood while officers' was painted a shade known as ivory gloss excepting bathrooms which were green, and a green paint said to contain arsenic (which would kill vermin!) was used for all ratings' and petty officers' cabins, washrooms, messrooms and alleyways. This green-painted crew accommodation was bare steel sprinkled with cork granules to combat condensation. The large emergency steering wheel was in the crew messroom.

Maximum speed was 15 knots. The maiden voyages were made on their designated trade while war clouds gathered, until the long anticipated outbreak brought this almost idyllic seafaring life to an abrupt end. September 1939 saw the entire fleet beginning to appear in uniform battleship grey, an early and quite effective camouflage which helped to make ships at sea less conspicuous to the enemy in those pre-radar days. With many of the company's larger vessels assigned to fast convoys, destinations including Malta, the three 'C's were diverted from the West Coast trade to wherever they became needed.

War service

First of the trio to see action was the *Canadian Star* in the North Atlantic on 20th July 1941. Outward bound from Liverpool towards New Zealand via Curacao and Panama, sailing unescorted under the command of Captain C.J.W. Jones, steering a zig zag course, she was attacked by U 203 during the middle watch, a dark clear night in good weather. Watchkeeping chief officer Percival Herbert Hunt (George to his friends) spotted the luminous track of a torpedo speeding towards them on the port beam. Ordering hard a'starboard he called the master and all hands by ringing the alarm bells and asked the engine room for maximum speed. That first torpedo missed, as did a second, then the submarine was seen on the surface, closing. A gun battle followed as the *Canadian Star* kept the U-boat right astern to minimise her target profile while working up to a speed far exceeding 15 knots. One of the German shells hit the ship's funnel causing an incandescent fire, highlighting her as a target, but good shooting by the stern gunners caused the submarine to discontinue the engagement and disappear. The ship had suffered several direct hits but not one of her people was injured and Captain Jones and his men were, in an official Admiralty letter, highly commended for their night's work .

Good luck was not to last, however. Homeward with a full cargo towards Liverpool from Australia and New Zealand, convoy routed via New York, her master was now Captain R.D. Miller with Mr Hunt still chief officer, Mr E.G. Buckwell still chief engineer. The 42-ship convoy left New York on 8th March 1943 and turned north after crossing the Newfoundland Banks, hoping to avoid the submarines which were by this time hunting in packs, voracious as wolves. The weather steadily deteriorated but this did not seem to deter the U-boats who had clearly worked out a plan calculated to cause maximum havoc within the convoy. Attacks continued for days and nights on end, one of the worst maulings experienced on the North Atlantic. By the 18th a north westerly gale was raising a tremendous sea

Canadian Star, 8th March 1943. *(United States Coast Guard/Ian Farquhar collection]*

and swell and while struggling to make seven knots, at 2.38 p.m. the ship ahead was torpedoed. By sheering off to starboard *Canadian Star* averted a collision but the submarine's periscope was spotted close on the port beam just before two torpedoes slammed into her also. German records later revealed these were fired by U 221. The torpedoes struck number 5 hold and the engine room respectively causing the vessel, mortally damaged, to begin to sink. Both port side boats, their luffing davits swung out on in accordance with wartime custom to expedite lowering, were blown to pieces in the explosions.

Captain Miller was killed after doing all he could to get people safely off the stricken ship and Mr Hunt took charge, ensuring passengers and crew got away in the remaining two boats and liferafts. However, number 3 boat capsized after a difficult launching in the heavy sea running, so as many survivors as could be found were accommodated in the remaining number 1 lifeboat, or aboard such rafts as still floated.

All survivors were clear of the ship by 3 p.m. just ten minutes before she sank by the stern, the bows hanging vertical above the heaving sea for minutes until finally taking the plunge. The survivors were picked up within two hours by H.M Corvettes *Anemone* and *Pennywort*. By the time they were landed at Gourock on 22nd March, 32 of the 91 aboard the *Canadian Star* when she was torpedoed had died, but that so many had survived in the weather prevailing was little short of miraculous. For his valiant efforts in saving so many lives, George' Hunt was awarded a well deserved M.B.E. After the war he became the company's chief marine superintendent.

Only two weeks before the *Canadian Star* was sunk her sister *California Star*, commanded by Captain Syd Foulkes, met a similar fate at the hands of U 515. Sailing unescorted homeward bound in mid Atlantic, north west of the Azores, around 7.30 p.m. - just after dark - in good weather, she was torpedoed twice on the starboard side just forward of the bridge. Both starboard side lifeboats were smashed, by the blast and the columns of water thrown up. The port side boats were lowered - number 4 safely but just as number 2 was three quarters down to the water a third torpedo struck immediately beneath it, wrecking the boat and killing all the occupants. Captain Foulkes was last to leave the ship. Diving overboard from the starboard side of the seaswept foredeck he swam towards a tiny light bobbing in the water which turned out to be a raft supporting the chief officer, third wireless operator and two gunners. As he was being hauled aboard a fourth torpedo hit the ship on the port side causing her to sink a few minutes later. From the first torpedo striking to taking the final plunge had taken only 30 minutes. The submarine surfaced and cruised around for a while, taking the second officer from a floating raft on board as a prisoner

California Star [Ian Farquhar collection]

Columbia Star 13th November 1943. *[United States Coast Guard/Ian Farquhar collection]*

of war. Rafts and boat managed to remain together. Came the dawn and the situation was assessed and discussed, it being decided that Captain Foulkes should transfer to the boat and sail her to Flores, approximately 380 miles to the south east. The rafts were tied together, given a share of food and water and, with Dr Erik Pedersen tending the wounded, were left to await rescue. The boat reached Flores eleven days later with 24 people onboard and Captain Foulkes gave the authorities the rafts' last known position. A vessel was sent to search but neither rafts nor survivors were ever found. Of the ship's complement of 74, only 23 survived this ordeal.

The sole survivor

Compared with her two sisters the *Columbia Star* led such a charmed life that she is not even mentioned in the company's wartime annals, except as one of the vessels surviving. I joined her as one of two first-voyage cadets at 24 Shed, Royal Albert Dock, London on 19th May 1951. She had never carried cadets before and we found ourselves in a newly furbished room, originally the chief officer's cabin. He had moved up a deck into the original doctor's room. Not yet settled on her originally intended West Coast of North America service, her previous voyage had been to Australia while my first trip was to South America. Our discharge ports were Rio de Janeiro, Santos, Montevideo and Buenos Aires, loading for Liverpool at San Sebastian Bay (Tierra del Fuego), Deseado (in Patagonia) and Buenos Aires, with Tenerife for bunkers in both directions.

But our following two voyages were from Newport (then in Monmouthshire) via Caracas Bay, Curacao, for bunkers, through the Panama Canal to Vancouver. So smartly was she maintained that the American Panama Canal pilot asked the captain if she were on her maiden voyage. (By this time she was 13 years old!) At each west coast port much was made of the ship's re-entry to the trade. Captain M.B.M. Tallack O.B.E. with his chief officer and chief steward - all veterans of Blue Star wartime sinkings - were interviewed on local radio in Vancouver, where the kindly citizens gave us all a marvellous time.

Much of our cargo from Newport consisted of big iron pipes for the Alberta oilfields while homeward

Dryden, ex Columbia Star. [Ships in Focus]

Above: *Columbia Star.* *[J. & M.Clarkson collection]*

Right: *Columbia Star* with no name on her bow and a plain funnel, perhaps in the course of being renamed *Dryden* ? *[W.H.Brown/J.& M.Clarkson collection]*

Below: *Patagonia Star*, the former *Columbia Star.* *[J. & M.Clarkson collection]*

we carried zinc ingots, apples, cases of Californian raisins, timber and borax with New Westminster, Seattle, Portland, San Francisco, Stockton and Los Angeles completing our schedule of leisurely loading. The following voyage was similar, sailing from Newport, then I left in 1953 to join another ship and the *Columbia Star* transferred to Lamport and Holt as the *Dryden*. The previous *Dryden* had the year before come to Blue Star as the *Fremantle Star*, changing to *Catalina Star* in 1958 when a new *Fremantle Star* was proposed.

The two old and highly respected Liverpool companies of Lamport and Holt and Booth Line were absorbed into the Vestey empire soon after the Second World War, their fleets having been sadly depleted in the conflict, their owners wishing to sell up while, if possible, still retaining identity. To enable them, and Blue Star Line, run the most suitable liners on their various and far reaching cargo-passenger services, a pool of ships was operated. This led to a frequent and somewhat bewildering series of name and colour changes which the uninitiated found hard to understand but it kept the two smaller companies operating as separate entities for another fifty years while availing Blue Star of such of their tonnage as may be required at short notice. Lamports prided themselves on having got their paint system down to three colours: black, white and blue, with white line between black boot topping and black topsides, but this differed considerably from Blue Star and Booth Line who had changed their hull topsides to grey when the Belgian (grey hull) *Thysville* became Booth Line's *Anselm* in 1961. (*Anselm* became *Iberia Star*, fifth ship on the regular London-South American service in 1963, transferring to the Vestey's Singapore Austasia Line as *Australasia* two years later. I sailed as her chief officer in 1969)

With a revival of the southern South America frozen lamb trade on which I had made my first voyage, *Columbia Star/Dryden* became the *Patagonia Star* in 1955. By 1957 she was again the *Columbia Star* but ended her days at Kaohsiung shipbreakers in 1968 as the *Dryden*, which she had been since yet another renaming five years earlier. (She certainly was a versatile, useful little ship!) Each name change was accompanied by an appropriate change of colours. I saw her in Liverpool before she sailed for Taiwan, as immaculate as she had ever been. No wonder, with all those coats of paint!

ANATOLI SEROV
ex John Holt

In his feature on John Holt in 'Record' 10, Geoff Holmes stated that the first *John Holt* of 1926, later the *Garthorpe*, had been sold to the USSR in 1939 and renamed *Anatoli Serov*. Geoff quoted a report from 1951 that the *Antoli Serov* had sunk in the Black Sea after striking a floating mine in 1949.

However, in May 2002 the 'Mersey Log' of the Merseyside Branch of the World Ship Society included photographs of the *Anatoli Serov* downloaded from a website. These were taken in Siberia around December 2001 by Nikolay Pritulyak and showed that the former *John Holt* was still in existence. She had been a fish transport registered at Petropavlovsk-Kamchatskiy.

Geoff asked for help finding the photographs of *Anatoli Serov* on the Internet. For assistance, we turned to reader Rick Cox of Cardiff, and soon both he and Ron Mapplebeck of Tees-side had located the website, which showed the photographs reproduced to the right. Photographs have also appeared of the interior wood panelling on the ship and of a Soviet survey certificate from 1956. This shows she was undoubtedly the same vessel and still steaming in 1956 as her engines and boilers were surveyed for class at Shanghai in September of that year. *Anatoliy Serov* still had her Middlesbrough-built triple expansion engine but had been reboilered with a pair of Belgian-built boilers of 1953 which may indicate when she was returned to service after being mined..The website's address is http://www.merchantships. click 2site.com/ NP.html

FONTEINS TO SOUTH AFRICA: Part 2

Peter Newall

Fleet list

BLOEMFONTEIN (1) 1920-1924
Twin screw
O.N. 123658 4,081g 2,602n 370.1 x 46.1 x 22.8 feet.
T. 3-cyl. by Wallsend Slipway Co. Ltd., Newcastle; 564 NHP, 14 knots.
Passengers: 100 first and 70 second; 1922: 90 first and 52 second.
12.12.1898: Launched by Sir Raylton Dixon & Co. Ltd., Middlesbrough (Yard No. 457) for African Steamship Company, Liverpool as CLARENCE.
18.5.1899: Completed as ANVERSVILLE for African Steamship Company's subsidiary Compagnie Belge Maritime du Congo S.A. Registered in Antwerp.
1.3.1906: Transferred to African Steamship Company (Elder, Dempster & Co.), Liverpool, renamed DAKAR and registered at London.
29.3.1915: Caught fire at Forcados, Nigeria and later declared a constructive total loss.
7.1917: Refloated and towed to Lagos.
8.1918: Taken over by the British Government and in management of The Shipping Controller.
1920: Sold to N.V. Nederlandsche Zuid-Afrikaansche Stoomvaart Maatschappij, Rotterdam. Repaired at Goole by Goole Shipbuilding & Reparing Co. Ltd.
1921: Renamed BLOEMFONTEIN and registered at Amsterdam.
1924: Sold to Ho Hong Steamship Co. Ltd. (Lim Kiang Beng), Singapore. Renamed HONG PENG and registered at Singapore.
1942: Became an ammunition hulk at Trincomalee.
7.1946: returned to owners.
3.1947: Broken up at Bombay.

JAGERSFONTEIN (1) 1920-1932
6,081g 3,906n 407.3 x 51.1 x 30.1 feet.
T. 3-cyl. by builder; 553 NHP, 11 knots.
8.1918: Completed by Osaka Iron Works Ltd., Osaka (Yard No. 901) for Katsuda Kisen K.K., Mitsugahama as KAIYEI MARU.
1920: Sold to N.V. Nederlandsche Zuid-Afrikaansche Stoomvaart Maatschappij, Rotterdam, renamed JAGERSFONTEIN and registered at Amsterdam.
1932: Sold to Tramp Shipping Development Co. Ltd. (Rethymnis & Kulukundis, Ltd.), Panama and renamed MOUNT HELIKON.
1935: Registration changed to Piraeus.
1936: Sold to Kulukundis Bros. S.A., Piraeus
1938: Owners restyled into Kulukundis Shipping Company S.A., Piraeus
1952: Sold to Leonidas G. Keranis (Goulandris Bros., managers.), Piraeus.
26.7.1953: Arrived at Port Glasgow for demolition by Smith & Houston Ltd.

RIETFONTEIN (1) 1921-1934
5,890g 3,746n 407.2 x 50.8 x 32.5 feet.
T. 3-cyl. by builder; 553 NHP, 11 knots.
Passengers: 20 first and 10 second; 1925: 25 first.
12.1918 : Completed by Osaka Iron Works Ltd., Osaka (Yard No. 898) for Uchida Kisen K.K., Osaka as TAIYU MARU.
1920: Sold to N.V. Van der Eb & Dresselhuy's Scheepvaart Maatschappij, Rotterdam and renamed MARISTO.
1921: Sold to N.V. Nederlandsche Zuid-Afrikaansche Stoomvaart Maatschappij, Rotterdam, renamed RIETFONTEIN.
1924: Registered at Amsterdam.
1932: Ownership changed to N.V. Vereenigde Nederlandsche Scheepvaart Maatschappij, The Hague.
10.6.1934: Arrived Rotterdam for demolition at Henrik-Ido-Ambacht by Frank Rijsdijk's Industrieele Ondernemingen N.V.

Opposite: The first *Bloemfontein* (1) was too small and remained in the fleet for only four years *[Ian Shiffman collection].* Above: *Jagersfontein* (1) was the only cargo-only *–fontein [Gerrit de Boer collection]* and later became *Mount Helikon*, seen here in the Mersey 6th June 1939 *[John McRoberts/J & M Clarkson collection]*. Below: Her sister *Rietfontein* (1) carried 30 passengers and is seen leaving Cape Town on 26th May 1933. *[The late Alex Duncan]*.

RANDFONTEIN (1)/RANDKERK 1921-1947
5,059g 3,159n 409.0 x 53.8 x 27.9 feet.
T. 3-cyl.. by Rankin & Blackmore Ltd., Greenock; 565 NHP, 11.5 knots.
Passengers: 22 first and 11 second; 1925: 30.
10.1920 : Completed by Greenock Dockyard Ltd., Greenock (Yard No. 400) for A/S Glittre (Fearnley & Eger), Christiania as STAUR.
1.1921: Sold to N.V. Nederlandsche Zuid-Afrikaansche Stoomvaart Maatschappij, Rotterdam, renamed RANDFONTEIN and registered at Amsterdam.
1925: Rebuilt at Hamburg.
1932: Ownership changed to N.V. Vereenigde Nederlandsche Scheepvaart Maatschappij, The Hague.
5.1940: Taken over by Nederlandsche Scheepvaart en Handelscommissie and managed by Phs. Van Ommeren (London) Ltd.
1.10.1945: Returned to owners.
10.1947: Passenger accommodation removed and renamed RANDKERK.
13.6.1950: Sold to N.V. Holland and arrived Rotterdam 29.6 in tow of the Dutch tug *Ganges* for demolition at Henrik-Ido-Ambacht in first quarter 1952.

Top: *Randfontein* (1). *[Gerrit de Boer collection]*
Middle: *Randfontein* (1) in wartime colours with gun mounted aft. *[Gerrit de Boer collection]*
Lower: At Cape Town in February 1948 as *Randkerk* and after her passenger accommodation had been removed. *[The late Alex Duncan].*

SPRINGFONTEIN 1921-1941
7,349g 5,532n 423.3 x 56.0 x 36.8 feet.
T. 3-cyl. by Rankin & Blackmore Ltd., Greenock; 565 NHP, 11 knots.
Passengers: 31 first; later increased to 28 first, 9 second and 60 steerage.
28.9.1921: Launched by Lithgows Ltd., Port Glasgow (Yard No. 733) for N.V. Nederlandsche Zuid-Afrikaansche Stoomvaart Maatschappij, Rotterdam as SPRINGFONTEIN. Acquired on the stocks.
12.1921: Completed and registered at Amsterdam.
1932: Ownership changed to N.V. Vereenigde Nederlandsche Scheepvaart Maatschappij, The Hague.
5.1940: Taken over by Nederlandsche Scheepvaart en Handelscommissie, London and managed by Phs. Van Ommeren (London) Ltd.
1.1.1941: On voyage Mombasa-UK via Cape Town with general cargo, caught fire at Freetown. Beached next day in Sierra Leone River and sank.

KLIPFONTEIN (1) 1922-1935
7,063g 4,423n 402.4 x 58.3 x 34.6 feet.
Two geared steam turbines by Metropolitan Vickers Electric Co, Manchester; 3,200 SHP, 12 knots.
Passengers: 20 first and 10 second.
8.2.1921: Launched by N.V. De Rotterdamsche Droogdok Maatschappij, Rotterdam (Yard No. 79) for N.V. Nederlandsche Zuid-Afrikaansche Stoomvaart Maatschappij, Rotterdam as KLIPFONTEIN.
10.4.1922: Completed and registered at Amsterdam.
1932: Ownership changed to N.V. Vereenigde Nederlandsche Scheepvaart Maatschappij, The Hague.
7.1935: Sold to Fratelli Giuseppe & Salvatore Rizzuto, Rome and renamed GLORIASTAR.
1936: Renamed GLORIASTELLA.
17.9.1940: Inbound from Naples, sunk by British aircraft from carrier H.M.S. ILLUSTRIOUS at Bengazi.
1949: Wreck raised.
2.1950: Broken up at La Spezia.

Springfontein. [Gerrit de Boer collection]

Springfontein. [Gerrit de Boer collection]

Klipfontein (1), the company's first Dutch-built ship. [Gerrit de Boer collection]

Top: *Nieuwkerk* as built in the Victoria Basin, Cape Town. *[The late Alex Duncan]*

Middle and lower: Minus her funnel, *Boschfontein* during lengthening and fitting with a Maierform bow. *[both Gerrit de Boer collection]*

Opposite top: *Boschfontein* as an US Navy transport and opposite lower, in the 1950s. *[both Gerrit de Boer collection]*

NIEUWKERK/BOSCHFONTEIN/ BOSCHKERK 1928-1958 Twin screw
6,280g 3,723n 410.9 x 59.5 x 27.2 feet.
Two geared steam turbines by Gebr. Stork & Co., Hengelo; 825 NHP, 3,500 SHP, 13 knots.
Passengers: 52 first; 1934 88 first; 1947: 79 first and 64 tourist; 1956: 12 first.
14.7.1928: Launched by N.V. Machinefabriek & Scheepswerf van P. Smit Jr., Rotterdam (Yard No. 418) for N.V. Vereenigde Nederlandsche Scheepvaart Maatschappij, The Hague as NIEUWKERK.
15.10.1928: Completed.
1934: Rebuilt by N.V Koninklijke Maatschappij 'De Schelde', Vlissingen and re-engined with two Sulzer-type 10-cyl. 2SCSA oil engines by builder, 1,705 NHP, 8,400 BHP, 16 knots.
16.7.1934: Towed to Rotterdam. Lengthened and given Maierform bow. New measurements: 7,139g 4,292n 453.7 x 59.5 x 27.2 feet.
17.8.1934: Towed to Vlissingen for finalizing refurbishment. Renamed BOSCHFONTEIN.
17.11.1934: Re-entered service.
9.1939: Chartered to Java-Pacific Line (N.V. Rotterdamsche Lloyd, Rotterdam).
1.6.1940: Taken over by Nederlandsche Scheepvaart en Handelscommissie, London and registered at Batavia.
1.3.1942: Management changed to N.V. Vereenigde Nederlandsche Scheepvaart Maatschappij, San Francisco
1.11.1942: Management changed to N.V. Stoomvaart Maatschappij 'Nederland', New York and chartered to U.S. War Shipping Administration.
1942: Converted into a 1,227-capacity transport for the US Navy and operated mainly in the Pacific based in San Francisco.
15.1.1946: Returned to owners.
7.9.1947: Damaged by fire at Amsterdam.
11.9.1947: Arrived at N.V. Amsterdamsche Droogdok Maatschappij for repairs and rebuilding.
1956: Most of passenger accommodation removed.
27.11.1956: Renamed BOSCHKERK.
19.10.1958: Engine room fire at Rotterdam.
26.12.1958: Arrived under tow at Hamburg for demolition by Eckhardt & Co. G.m.b.H.

Right: Showing off her extraordinary Maierform bow, *Bloemfontein* (2) prior to launching.

Below: With her superstructure extended aft, *Bloemfontein* (2) outward-bound in the Noordzee Canal circa 1950. *[both Gerrit de Boer collection]*

BLOEMFONTEIN (2) **1934-1959**
Twin screw
10,081g 6,160n 457.2 x 63.3 x 34.9 feet.
Two 6-cyl 2SCDA oil engines by Gebr. Stork & Co., Hengelo; 8,300 BHP, 16.5 knots
Passengers: 93 first and 32 steerage; 1947: 111 first and 66 tourist.
16.6.1934: Launched by N.V Nederlandsche Scheepsbouw Maatschappij, Amsterdam (Yard No. 228) for N.V. Vereenigde Nederlandsche Scheepvaart Maatschappij, The Hague as BLOEMFONTEIN.
18.10.1934: Completed.
9.1939: Chartered to Java Pacific Line (N.V. Stoomvaart Maatschappij 'Nederland', Amsterdam).
1.6.1940: Taken over by Nederlandsche Scheepvaart en Handelscommissie and registered at Batavia.
13.4.1942: Entered service as a 2,334-capacity transport for the US Navy and operated mainly in the Pacific based in San Francisco. Chartered to US War Shipping Administration.
10.4.1945: Returned to owners and chartered to the Dutch Government.
1947: Rebuilt at Amsterdam by Nederlandsche Dok- & Scheepsbouw Maatschappij.
13.9.1947: Re-entered service.
4.1959: Sold.
8.8.1959: Arrived Hong Kong for demolition.

JAGERSFONTEIN (2) 1934-1942
Twin screw
10,083g 6,164n 457.2 x 63.3 x 34.9 feet.
Two 6-cyl 2SCDA oil engines by Gebr. Stork & Co., Hengelo; 8,300 BHP, 16.5 knots
Passengers: 93 first and 32 steerage
18.12.1934: Launched by N.V Nederlandsche Scheepsbouw Maatschappij, Amsterdam (Yard No. 229) for N.V. Vereenigde Nederlandsche Scheepvaart Maatschappij, The Hague as JAGERSFONTEIN.
16.12.1934: Completed.
9.1939: Chartered to Java Pacific Line (N.V. Stoomvaart Maatschappij 'Nederland', Amsterdam).
1.6.1940: Taken over by Nederlandsche Scheepvaart en Handelscommissie and registered at Batavia.
26.6.1942: On voyage Galveston-Liverpool torpedoed and sank by German submarine U 107 495 miles east of Bermuda in position 31.56 north by 54.48 west. All aboard were rescued by Swiss freighter ST. CERGUE (4,260/1937).

Top: *Jagersfontein* (2) with Dutch neutral markings.

Both *Bloemfontein* (2) and *Jagersfontein* (2) carried just under a 100 first class passengers in very comfortable accommodation. The dining saloon on *Jagersfontein (2)* was situated forward on D-deck with large sea-view windows (right top) and above this, on the Promenade Deck, was the main lounge or social hall (right middle) which opened, at the forward end, onto the palm court and dance floor (right bottom). *[all Gerrit de Boer collection]*

Top: *Klipfontein* (2) on charter to the Java-Pacific Line
Bottom: As a US Navy transport. *[both Gerrit de Boer collection]*
The interior design of *Klipfontein* (2) was a Dutch version of art deco. The beautiful use of wood and metal can be clearly seen in the main first class entrance on A-deck (top right) and the handsome first class library and writing room on the Promenade Deck. *[both Peter Newall collection]*
Bottom right: the last moments of *Klipfontein* (2). *[Gerrit de Boer collection]*.

KLIPFONTEIN 1939-1953 Twin screw
10,544g 6,321n 499.3 x 62.9 x 33.1 feet.
Two Burmeister & Wain-type 5-cyl. 2SCDA oil engines by builders; 11,800BHP, 17.5 knots
Passengers: 106 first and 42 tourist; 1948: 130 first and 68 tourist
4.3.1939: Launched by N.V. Machinefabriek & Scheepswerf van P. Smit Jr., Rotterdam (Yard No. 517) for N.V. Vereenigde Nederlandsche Scheepvaart Maatschappij, The Hague as KLIPFONTEIN.
11.7.1939: Completed.
17.10.1939: Chartered to the Java-Pacific Line (N.V. Rotterdamsche Lloyd, Rotterdam).
1.6.1940: Taken over by Nederlandsche Scheepvaart en Handelscommissie and registered at Batavia.
23.2.1942: Entered service as a 1,981-capacity transport for the US Navy and operated mainly in the Pacific based in San Francisco. Chartered to US War Shipping Administration.
1.2.1946: Returned to owners.
15.1.1947: Re-entered service.
1.8.1947: Arrived at Amsterdam for rebuilding by Nederlandsche Dok- & Scheepsbouw Maatschappij.
8.1.1952: On voyage Lourenço Marques-Beira struck submerged rocks five miles from Cape Barra near Inhambane, Moçambique in position 24.32 south by35.14 east. All passengers and crew rescued by BLOEMFONTEIN CASTLE (18,400/1949).

ORANJEFONTEIN 1945-1967
Twin screw
10,547g 6,299n 499.3 x 62.9 x 33.1 feet.
Two Burmeister & Wain-type 5-cyl. 2SCDA oil engines by builders; 11,800BHP, 17.5 knots
Passengers: 160 first 60 tourist
21.3.1940: Launched by N.V. Machinefabriek & Scheepswerf van P. Smit Jr., Rotterdam (Yard No. 532) for N.V. Vereenigde Nederlandsche Scheepvaart Maatschappij, The Hague as ORANJEFONTEIN.
20.12.1940: Completed.
17.3.1941: Seized by German Navy.
23.6.1941: Became target for the Luftwaffe.
28.8.1941: Damaged at Rotterdam by British aircraft.
21.10.1941: Transferred to 27th U-Boot Flotille.
1945: Used to transport refugees from German eastern territories in the Baltic. Reported as having name changed to PIONEER. Deutsche Ost-Afrika-Linie, Hamburg became managers.
12.7.1945: Handed over to the Dutch Government at Kiel, and rebuilt at Newcastle for voyage to Australia via Dutch East-Indies.
1.2.1946: Arrived at Rotterdam for rebuild by N.V. Machinefabriek & Scheepswerf van P. Smit Jr.
20.4.1946: Entered service.
21.9.1959: Badly damaged in River Scheldt in collision with Norwegian HAVTROLL (5,169/1956).
6.1967: Laid up at Rotterdam.
11.8.1967: Arrived at Bilbao as FONTEIN for demolition.

Top: *Oranjefontein* was launched just seven weeks before the invasion of Holland.
Middle: *Oranjefontein*. Cranes forward distinguish her from her near-sister *Jagersfontein* (2).
Bottom: On her way to the breakers as *Fontein. [all Gerrit de Boer collection]*

Right: *Elandsfontein* was launched a week after *Oranjefontein*. After two years sunk in the River Vistula she was raised (note the watermark along her side) and towed to Holland in August 1947. She was completed as *Jagersfontein* (2) and is seen at Cape Town in August 1952. *[bottom the late Alex Duncan , others Gerrit de Boer collection]*.

ELANDSFONTEIN/JAGERSFONTEIN (2) 1950-1967 Twin screw
10,547g 6,308n 499.1 x 62.8 x 33.0 feet.
Two Sulzer-type 9-cyl. 2SCSA oil engines by builders; 12,000BHP, 17.5 knots
Passengers: 146 first, 60 tourist
30.3.1940: Launched by F. Schichau G.m.b.H., Danzig (Yard No. 1,441) for N.V. Vereenigde Nederlandsche Scheepvaart Maatschappij, The Hague as ELANDSFONTEIN. Laid down as RIETFONTEIN (2). Work ceased soon afterwards and she was laid up.
14.3.1945: Shelled by the Russian army and sank in the River Vistula.
20.3.1947: Wreck was raised.
15.5.1947: Released by the Russian authorities.
2.8.1947: Departed Danzig in tow of Dutch tug ZWARTE ZEE for completion by N.V Koninklijke Maatschappij 'De Schelde', Vlissingen.
11.3.1950: Completed as JAGERSFONTEIN.
5.1967: Laid up at Rotterdam
11.1967: Sold to Embajade Compania Naviera S.A. (N. Kulukundis, Piraeus), Panama and renamed DEVON for final voyage.
23.12.1967: Arrived at Kaohsiung for demolition.

Randfontein arriving at Cape Town fully-laden in October 1959. *[Albert Newall]*

RANDFONTEIN (2) 1958-1970
Twin screw
13,694g 7,971n 584.5 x 70.2 x 29.5 feet.
Two M.A.N-Werf-type 9-cyl. 2SCSA oil engines by builders; 15,400BHP, 18.5 knots
Passengers: 123 first and 174 tourist; 1971 122 cabin class and 142 tourist.
28.6.1958: Floated out by Dok- en Werf Maatschappij Wilton-Fijnoord N.V., Schiedam (Yard No. 760) for N.V. Vereenigde Nederlandsche Scheepvaart Maatschappij, The Hague as RANDFONTEIN.
6.12.1958: Commissioned.
6.1.1959: Maiden voyage Amsterdam-South Africa.
1.7.1970: Owner changed to Koninklijke Nedlloyd N.V., Rotterdam.
3.9.1971: Arrived Rotterdam on last voyage from South Africa. Transferred to Koninklijke Java-China Paketvaart Lijnen N.V., Amsterdam and renamed NIEUW HOLLAND. Rebuilt by N.V Koninklijke Maatschappij 'De Schelde', Vlissingen.
20.1.1972: Maiden voyage from Hong Kong to Japan and Australia.
27.11.1974: Sold to Yick Fung Shipping & Enterprises Co. (Hong Kong) for China Ocean Shipping Company Ltd., Shanghai and in 1975 renamed YU HUA.
1981: Renamed HAI XING.
1984: Sold to Shanghai Hai Xing Shipping Company Ltd., Shanghai.
1991-1996: Laid up at Hong Kong.
13.6.1996: Arrived at Alang, India under St.Vincent flag for demolition as HERBERT.

As *Nieuw Holland* she was fitted with a large crane forward. *[Gerrit de Boer collection]*

She was sold to COSCO in 1974 and became *Yu Hua*. Note the radar mast attached to her funnel. *[Gerrit de Boer collection]*

PUTTING THE RECORD STRAIGHT

Letters, additions, amendments and photographs relating to articles in any issues of *Record* are welcomed. Letters may be lightly edited. E-mails are welcome, but senders are asked to include their postal address.

In *'Record'* 4 page 242 it is stated that in 1937 the *Mosholu* was the last square rigger to load at Port Adelaide. This is not so as that distinction belongs to the *Lawhill*. When attending the A.I.C.H. Congress at St. Malo last May I spoke to a man who served in the *Lawhill* all the time she was under the South African flag following her seizure as a prize of war. He assured me that they loaded wheat three times at Port Adelaide in the early 1940s.
A.R.C. ORMOND, 3 Belle Vue Place, Unley Park, South Australia 5061, Australia

Iron Chief (2), purchased in 1930 to replace her namesake lost through stranding in 1928 ('Record' 25, page 55), spent most of her career laid up until sold to British owners in 1934, according to 'The Iron Ships: A Maritime History of BHP 1883-1992' (published by Broken Hill Proprietary Co. Ltd.). The first *Iron Chief* was built as the British collier *Maindy Lodge* and was renamed in 1922.
BOB SILBERBERG, 22 Ernest Street, Beauty Point, 7270, Tasmania, Australia.

Astrea ('Record' 28, page 218) was acquired by P/f Skipafelagid Føroyar, Torshavn in November 1967, but included in the sale was a bareboat contract for three months. The problem for the buyers was that she was far too old to be registered in Denmark. With the bareboat arrangement she could remain in the Norwegian Register. On 15th February 1968 she was taken over and her registry was transferred to Panama. This arrangement caused a great deal of newspaper discussion in Denmark about avoiding Nordic safety regulations and the ship was popularly known as the 'Panama *Tjaldur*'. On 18th July 1969,while northbound in the Kattegat, her old Krupp diesel engine broke down and she was towed back to Aalborg where she was laid up pending inspection. She was declared a constructive total loss and sold to be broken up.
SØREN THORSØE, 4 Magnolievangen, 3450 Allerød, Denmark

The article 'Wavecrest follow up' in 'Record' 28 showing the colour photos of *Skycrest*, failed to mention her sister-ship which Ivanovic Co. owned, *Southwick*. This class of ship deserves to have an article of its own because there were several built, albeit without the Stülcken, for such companies as Louis Dreyfus/Buries Markes and even C.Y.Tung (*Oriental Star*). It could have been France's answer to the SD 14, since they had a ten year start with *La Pradera*. It is surprising that they did not participate in the Liberty ship replacement programme with this design.
A.D. FROST, 32 Oakfield Close, Sunderland SR3 3RT

Way back in 'Record' 2 the caption to a photograph of the Goole Trader *on page 122 had the 1884-built former Goole Steam Shipping steamer broken up in 1928. George Robinson points out that this was not so. She was renamed* Tervsund *for other Finnish owners in 1929, and as this survived until 13th September 1947 when she stranded near Varberg during a ballast voyage from Landskrona to Middlesbrough.*

Whilst confessing to past errors, the editor has to admit not to referring back to facts printed in his own journal when suggesting on page 195 of 'Record' 28 that Vestris *was lost by fire in 1928, whereas the Lamport and Holt passenger steamer actually foundered. Full details are in the late Rowan Hackman's article in 'Record' 15.*

The *Magdalena* model

A short footnote to her very short career *('Record' 25)*. Royal Mail commissioned a very large display model of the ship (mentioned on page 125, *'Record'* 26). When *Magdalena* was lost this model was, understandably, not required and was given by Royal Mail to the Nautical College, Pangbourne. It was in the Seamanship Room between 1954 and 1958. The model was about six feet long and the top of the display case was about six feet from the floor. The interesting thing about the model was that it was not complete as some of the rigging had not been finished and some of the small fittings were also missing. The story we were told was that the model was not quite complete when she was lost and all work on it stopped immediately and Royal Mail gave it to Pangbourne as it was a major embarrassment to them. But in spite of this, it was a magnificent model and may still be at Pangbourne.
DAVID TRANTER, 1 Upgate, Poringland, Norwich NR14 7SH

Points on Poseidons

I could not let the story of 'The Poseidon Six' (*Record* 27) pass without some comments and observations, because those ships caught my attention soon after they entered service. Before going into detail, I would like to correct one or two facts in the article. Firstly, as can be seen from the photographs, the ships had six holds and six hatches, each hold having a 'tween deck. Secondly, apart from the six ships which entered service, two more of the same design were on order from Flensburg when war broke out. These ships were for delivery in 1940 but were cancelled. Nevertheless they were an indication of Hugo Stinnes' satisfaction with this particular design of ship.

A very minor correction - the Norwegian company which purchased the *Mulheim-Ruhr* in 1947, A/S Borgestad, have during their 99-year existence been based at Porsgrunn, not Oslo. It appears that the Poseidon ships were intended essentially for the coal and pulp-wood trades, although early in their careers they were trading to Canada and Cuba. As Craig Carter explains, four of the ships soon found profitable employment carrying cotton from the US Gulf to the River Mersey. In effect, they were tramp ships, but with two very innovative features: the substitution of deck cranes for derricks and the employment of twin diesel engines, reduction geared, to a single propeller shaft. Deck cranes had been used to a limited extent on German cargo liners but they were unknown on British tramp ships and only employed to a very limited extent on British cargo liners after the Second World War. Presumably the hesitancy to use cranes was based upon first cost and uncertainty regarding their reliability. But the eight six-ton Demag cranes on the Stinnes ships appear to have been satisfactory. It was ten years after the advent of the German ships before another series of ships using all deck cranes instead of derricks emerged. These were the Swedish Johnson Line *Seattle*-class cargo liners which were equipped with 12 deck cranes and no derricks. Clearly the arrangement must have given satisfaction, because the Swedish company later ordered seven similar ships for their River Plate trade. Today, the tables have turned completely because one never sees a ship equipped with derricks for handling cargo.

For some years prior to the Second World War German liner companies had to a limited extent used twin geared diesel engines in their ships, but this arrangement was not seen in tramp ships up to the building of the Stinnes ships. British tramp ship owners never really accepted geared diesels as a means of propulsion, but in recent years applications have been found in fast ferries and cruise liners, where space is limited and power requirements are high.

If one were to look for another innovation in the German ships it was the compact midships structure. It is interesting to note how the superstructure gradually became

more streamlined in successive ships until in the *Mulheim-Ruhr* it was actually oval in shape.
JOHN B. HILL, The Hollies, Wall, Hexham, Northumberland NE46 4EQ

Sobriquets supplied

Many congratulations on the team's latest 'Record'. As a point of interest re the former *Skycrest*, page 234 and back cover, the 'S' in her Greek name, and the white Sigma on the funnel mark, refer to Simbouras Brothers (Partners) Co. (A.& S.& D. Simbouras), Piraeus. Syros Shipping Co. (L.M. Valmas and Son) Ltd. were their London agents and a reciprocal arrangement applied in Piraeus.

Mr. Frost's notion of compiling a list of aliases for shipping company titles ('Record' 28) may turn up some novel or comical results but will no doubt fall foul of political correctness. Some acceptable examples are:

General Steam Navigation: 'The Navvies'
Henderson Line: 'Paddy' Henderson
Booth Line: 'Maggie' Booth
British Tanker Co. (BTC): 'Better Times Coming'
Esso Tankers: 'Eat, Sleep, Sweat & Overtime'

Funnel markings also gave rise to the following:

Trinder, Anderson & Co. (black swan on flag/funnel): 'hungry goose'
Bailey & Leetham (deep white verticals on black funnel): 'tombstone line'

Devices also attracted uncomplimentary descriptions:

Palm Line (palm tree): 'the green loo-brush'
Baltic Trading Co. (crossed hammer and flaming torch in red on white band): 'chipping hammer and red lead brush'

Crew origins, including:

Port Line: 'Stornoway navy'
Blue Funnel: 'Welsh navy'

Crew catering:

Pollock and Gilmour (predecessors of Mitchell, Cotts' Saint Line), known as 'poverty and grief', and of whom it was said of their sail fleet:
These are the ships of 'Poverty and Grief'
Quite a lot of bone, but not a lot of beef!
Lamport + Holt: 'lean + hungry'

Tatem's tramps got off more lightly with 'T on the funnel, but none on the table'. Hogarth's were asking for trouble with Hugh's initials on the houseflag, but my personal experience in *Baron Inverclyde* did not support the bad name they had acquired.
ALAN PHIPPS, 2 Riverside Road, Droitwich Spa, Worcestershire WR9 8UW

'D' for draughty

In 1949 I was second mate of Lamport and Holt's *Delane* ('Record' 28). I remember the external ladder on the starboard side that extended over two decks up to the bridge. The crew were not allowed to use the comfortable ladder within the funnel and negotiating this external ladder in a gale was a daunting exercise. To allow access to this ladder at bridge level a gap had to be left in the after bulwark. This resulted in the most cold and draughty bridge that I have ever known. Arctic winds came through that gap! This ladder is just visible on the photo of *Delane* but does not appear on any other 'D' class photograph. It is possible that this ladder was added in wartime, as without it the only way to reach or leave the bridge would be through the funnel. This could become inaccessible in the event of an accident or enemy action and it was a long way down to jump.

The single loop direction finder is clearly shown, mounted high above the top of the funnel. Down in the radio room a wheel, marked with relative bearing, rotated this loop. The wheel was connected to the single loop by a metal rod that passed through bearings in three decks. Through age, no doubt, there had been some slight movement between these decks that made it almost impossible to rotate the rod smoothly and thus obtain an accurate D/F bearing.

The ship looked magnificent in dry dock having very few flat plates in the hull. This promised a fast ship but the reality was 12 to 13 knots and a very small number 1 hold. The sheer aft was very small: early one morning a wave came aboard flooding the crews' quarters and setting forward the mooring wire reels including that of the insurance wire.

When I returned from leave in 1948, the bosun told me that his pay had gone up. The reason for this was not a result of his devotion and hard work, but that the ship had been converted from an open shelter deck to a closed shelter deck type. The resulting increase in her gross tonnage moved him up one grade in the tonnage-related pay scale.
M.D.A. LEE, 173 Barnes Lane, Sarisbury Green, Southampton S031 7BH

'Record' number 28 is as excellent as ever and I have now read every word. Those Lamport D boats were shockers. I never sailed in one but went aboard *Geelong Star* (ex-*Defoe*) in Geelong, visiting a friend of mine who was her second officer. He showed me that the only way up to the monkey island to take a compass bearing was by climbing up through a manhole trapdoor steel cover, and with a following wind you were then gassed by smoke from that ridiculously low funnel. Lamport and Holt left to themselves were not strong on ship maintenance: another pal of mine went as mate of the *Seattle Star* when she had just come over from Lamports

Alan Phipp's note about Bailey and Leetham's 'Tombstone Line' sobriquet prompts us to include this photograph of the company's *Vera* (2,019/1887), which was not illustrated in the Ships in Focus book on Bailey and Leetham. The short-lived ship was in the fleet only from January 1887, when acquired from French owners, until March 1889 when, as seen here, she ran onto Chesil Beach, Dorset and became a total loss. The photograph also shows the 'tombstone' particularly well. Copies of 'Bailey and Leetham' by Arthur Credland and Richard Greenwood are still available: the book provides a fascinating insight into the affairs of a nineteenth century shipowner. *[Photo courtesy John Bartlett]*

and at his first boat drill those radial davits bent under the strain of trying to lift the boats, which were firmly stuck in their chocks. Clearly they had not been properly swung out for years!

With due respect to Stephen Howells' article 'The Cunard Reefers', he does not mention *Saxonia's* Falklands STUFT service. (We were all STUFT ships taken up from trade.) You may be interested in the enclosed photograph. *Saxonia* was in Port Line colours for her Falklands Ministry of Defence charter but the red and black funnel does not show up well on the photo. When Trafalgar House bought Cunard and took Port Line away from its very cosy union with Blue Star, they immediately sold all the Port Line ships and declared a handsome profit - asset stripping at its worst. But when they then bought the reefers we optimistically thought Port Line was about to re-emerge. How wrong we were! Those ships too were shockers, especially the smaller ones. That large forecastle full of cargo made them VERY tender - always a stability problem, and they had a propensity for oil spills which made them very popular! The *Trojan Star* even lost her rudder, in heavy weather off New Zealand, and my pal Peter Daniel had quite a job to get her safely into Wellington. None of us were sorry to see them go.
CAPTAIN A.W. KINGHORN, 15 Kendal Avenue, Cullercoats, North Shields, Tyne and Wear NE30 3AQ

The unfortunate Cunard reefers
Seeing the references to the *Servia* reminded me of an incident when she was in collision with Blue Star Lines' *Almeria Star* in the waters off Zeebrugge during the early hours of 14th June 1984. My local contact, Bert Kruidhof, was able to position us near the Scheldeport entrance to view the *Almeria Star* arriving later that day for repairs, and the hole made by the bulbous bow of the *Servia* was clearly visible, along with other damage along the port side. This occurrence was possibly overshadowed by the publicity surrounding HMS *Jupiter* contacting London Bridge a few days earlier, but doubts were certainly being cast on the quality of Anglo-Saxon navigation when we subsequently visited the Vlissingen control tower.

I never did find out what the findings were on the circumstances of the collision, but a chance conversation with a retired master only last year (in a cafe off the A30) revealed his belief that, whatever the rights and wrongs at the time, sadly this event had effectively put an end to the career of his colleague who had been the *Servia's* skipper.
ROLAND WHAITE, 9 The Paddock, Chepstow, NP16 5BW

I have found the following references in the Annual Reports of Trafalgar House Limited relating to the Cunard Reefers.

1977 Our container interests continue to be the main source of profit, assisted now by the refrigerated fruit carriers and the Port Line conventional refrigerated ships.

1978 The fruit carriers charter to Salen has been extended for 12 months, but their performance is highly sensitive to the relative weakness of the dollar.

1979 Our principal burden consists of the fleet of refrigerated fruit carriers which operate in a near- static market to which unwanted tonnage has recently been introduced. These ships were brought when the dollar exchange rate was 1.65 to the pound, and on expiry of the original Salen charters were fixed with United Brands at levels very little higher than those prevailing three years ago.

1980 The fruit carriers continue under their two year charter to United Brands. This market still suffers from over capacity and virtually static market requirements, but there are now signs that the situation could improve during the next two years as other owners sell older ships for scrap. In the meantime, of course, the operation loses money.

1981 The four smaller fruit carriers were sold at a loss during the year when it became inescapably clear that there was no prospect of them being traded profitably in the foreseeable future. In the case of the six larger fruit carriers,

Saxonia on charter to The Ministry of Defence. See Captain Kinghorn's letter. *[King George's Fund for Sailors, published by Kenneth Mason]*

Almeria Star arrives at Scheldeport on 14th June 1984 with a crumpled hull following a collision with *Servia*. As Ian Farquhar's research into Cunard reports make clear, the whole reefer adventure was an unfortunate one for the Cunard Group. *[Roland Whaite]*

charters were extended for a further three years at rates reflecting a decided improvement.

1984 The time charter of the fruit carriers to United Brands is in its final stages, with two ships already having been redelivered. Whilst every effort has been and will continue to be made to secure employment for these ships prospects appear to be rather limited in the present difficult reefer market conditions.

1985 The market for refrigerated ships had deteriorated further and with little prospect of the ships trading profitably the decision was taken to terminate Cunard's involvement in this trade. Since 30 September 1985 the six ships have been sold.

It would appear that apart from providing employment to some Cunard Group officers, who would otherwise have been made redundant as the conventional fleets were replaced by container ships, the venture into reefer shipping was not very profitable.

IAN FARQUHAR, RD2, Dunedin, New Zealand

From Latvia to Scotland

May I comment briefly on two of the splendid articles in Record 27?

Captain Kinghorn's article includes a shot of the long-lived tramp *Lorna*: uncharacteristically, it shows her in rather a work-stained condition for she was normally kept very smart, despite her considerable age and her humdrum existence. She was quite a regular on the run from North Africa to Granton (on the Firth of Forth) with esparto grass and usually put in several appearances each year. Quite often she would then make the short ballast journey round to the Tyne to load coke (which, like esparto grass, involved the carriage of some of the cargo on deck) for Lisbon or Italy.

Part of the reason for her appearances in the Forth may have been that she was managed by Neil and Hannah of Leith, a firm which had owned ships before the war but was by then operating only in the agency and management business. Their pre-war operations had brought them into regular contact with the Baltic states, which may be why they had been chosen by the owners of the *Lorna* to manage the ship.

Captain Kinghorn tells us that even 'Lloyd's Confidential Index' gave no clues as to the true owners of the ship. I think, however, that he met some of them when he was on board the ship as my understanding at the time (when I was a teenager with relatives in the Leith shipping scene) was that her real owners were a group of Latvian exiles, some of whom were the officers and crew of the ship. Latvia (and its neighbours Estonia and Lithuania) had been independent republics between the two world wars. They were occupied by Russia in the early part of the Second World War, then invaded by Nazi Germany at the time that it began its Russian offensive, then forcibly recaptured by the Soviet Army in the closing stages of the war. Quite a number of the inhabitants of those countries fled to western Europe in the ghastly chaos after the war: some were given permits of residence but remained officially 'stateless' for many years. The owners of the *Lorna* could not, therefore, be an openly registered company as some of them had no officially-recognised nationality. For the same reason, I suspect that the ship could not participate in certain trades as the crew, some of whom lacked passports, would be treated hostilely in some countries.

My memory, incidentally, rings a bell that the crew were Estonian rather than Latvian but I may have got that wrong. I do, however, recall one incident from my schooldays in broad outline rather than in detail. I saw her one day discharging esparto grass and noticed that she was flying a strange flag at her stern; when I returned the next day to show my father, she had reverted to the Liberian flag. He was subsequently told that my first visit had been the National Day of the pre-war republic, and the old flag had been flown in remembrance. That was almost 50 years ago and I may have mis-remembered the whole thing! Her funnel colours were the blue-and-white cross of St Andrew (the Scottish national emblem) against several red-and-white bands (the background of the Liberian national flag), signifying the link between the two so far as this ship was concerned.

I much enjoyed the article by Graeme Somner on London Scottish Lines. May I correct a tiny, but uncharacteristic, error? He refers to the original owners of the *Edinburgh Merchant* as the Scottish Wholesale Co-operative Society. The two middle words have been transposed: in its trade slogans and advertising, the organisation often used simply its initials, which were SCWS.

COLIN MENZIES. 17 Bickenhall Mansions, London W1U 6BP

SOURCES AND ACKNOWLEDGEMENTS

We thank all who gave permission for their photographs to be used, and for help in finding photographs we are particularly grateful to Tony Smith, Jim McFaul and David Whiteside of the World Ship Photo Library; to Ian Farquhar, F.W. Hawks, Bill Laxon, Peter Newall, Ivor Rooke, William Schell, George Scott; and to David Hodge and Bob Todd of the National Maritime Museum, and other museums and institutions listed.

Research sources have included the *Registers* of William Schell and Tony Starke, *Lloyd's Register*, *Lloyd's Confidential Index*, *Lloyd's War Losses*, *Mercantile Navy Lists*, *Marine News* and *Shipbuilding and Shipping Record*. Use of the facilities of the World Ship Society's Central Record, the Guildhall Library, the Public Record Office and Lloyd's Register of Shipping are gratefully acknowledged. Particular thanks also to Heather Fenton for editorial and indexing work, and Marion Clarkson for accountancy services.

THE FURNESS WITHY - HOULDER BROTHERS LINK

The contribution of John B. Hill is gratefully acknowledged.

THE ARCH DECK STEAMERS

So many have contributed to this feature that 'The Archers' seems an appropriate attribution of its authorship. David Burrell began the project, identified the vessels, and located most of the technical literature, but it also drew on work by Harold Appleyard, Malcolm Cooper, Roy Fenton, Stig Lothner, Kevin O'Donoghue, Bill Schell, George Scott and the words of the designer himself, Maxwell Ballard.

The following published references to arch deck ships have been consulted.

Anonymous 'Arch Deck Steamer of 3,100 tons d.w. with 'Cruiser' Stern' *Shipbuilding and Shipping Record* 29th March 1917, page 295

Ballard, Maxwell 'A New Design of Merchant Vessel', *The Marine Engineer and Naval Architect*, July 1911, pages 402-405 and 457-460

Ballard, Maxwell 'The Design of Merchant Ships' *The Shipbuilder* 1913

Ballard, Maxwell letter in *Fairplay* 22nd September 1921

Ballard, Maxwell 'The Arch Principle of Ship Construction' *Shipbuilding and Shipping Record*, 10th May 1923, pages 612-614

Ballard, Maxwell 'The Arch Principle' *Sea Breezes* April 1953 page 305

Biographical notes on Ayre and Ballard in *Shipbuilding and Shipping Record* 4th September 1913, page 293 and 10th February 1916.

THE LAST SQUARE RIGGERS BUILT FOR BRITISH OWNERS

Information was kindly provided by Unilever Historical Archives, Merseyside Maritime Museum, Glasgow City Council and the University of Glasgow.

G000089528

Adding and Taking Away

Helping your child

- The activities in this book will help your child to learn about adding and taking away. Pictures provide hints and clues to support your child's calculations.
- Your child will gain the confidence to: read, write and identify numbers to 20; use a number line to count on and back; add and take away one-digit numbers to and from each other; understand the +, – and = symbols; and calculate the value of an unknown number within a number sentence.
- Your child will learn about numbers to 20, adding and subtracting bonds, counting, comparing and differences.
- Set aside time to do the activities together. Do a little at a time, so that your child enjoys learning.
- Give lots of encouragement and praise. Use the gold stars as rewards and incentives.
- The answers are on page 32.

This edition published by Parragon Books Ltd in 2017

Parragon Books Ltd
Chartist House
15-17 Trim Street
Bath BA1 1HA, UK
www.parragon.com

Written by Paul Broadbent
Illustrated by Adam Linley
Cover illustrated by Simon Abbot
Educational Consultant: Christine Vaughan

ISBN: 978-1-4748-7792-3

Printed in China

Contents

Numbers to 10

Trace the numbers. Join each kite to the right number. Join each number to the right group of pictures at the bottom of each page.

Note for parent: Ask your child to say each number and word aloud as he or she traces over them.

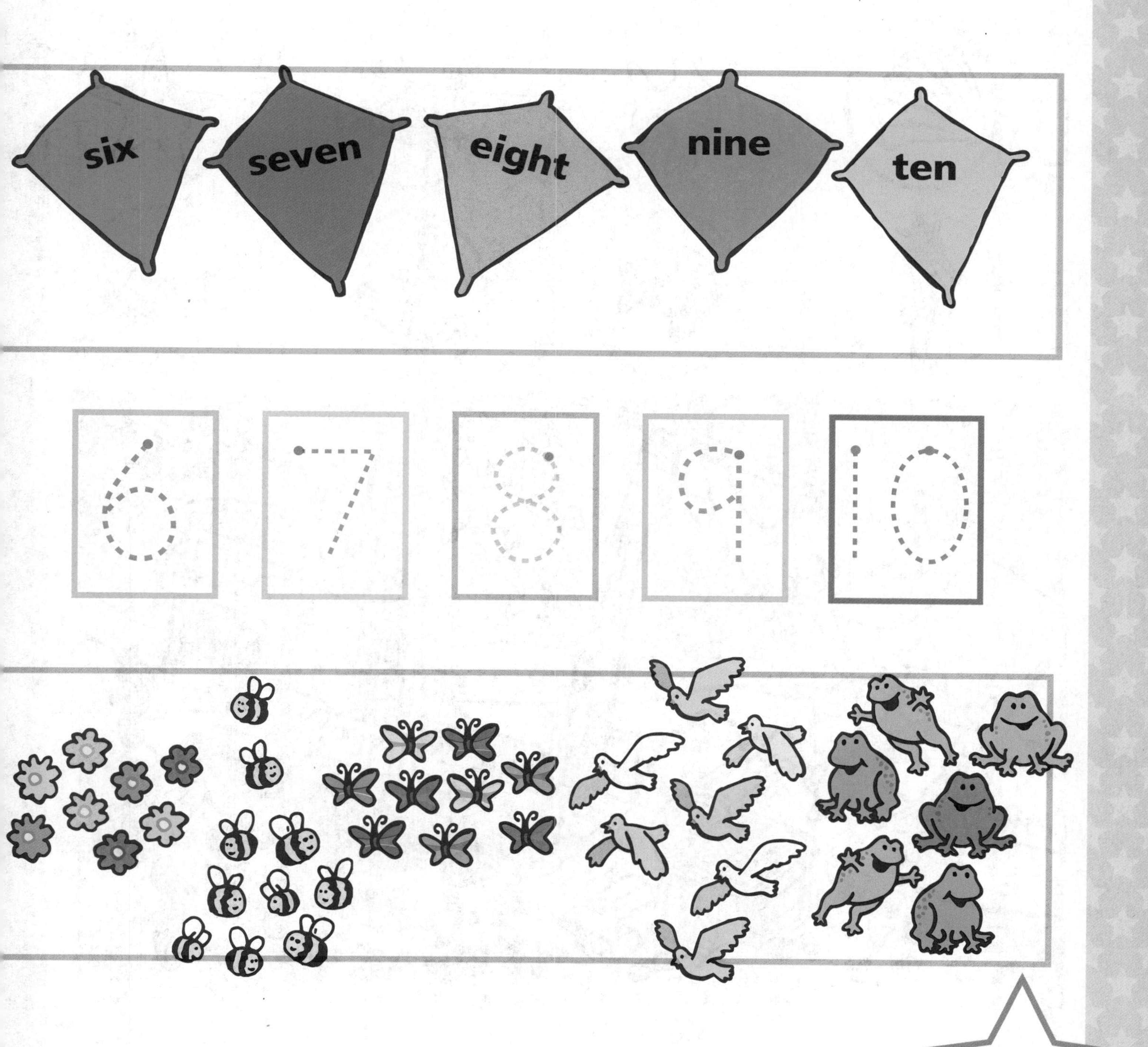

Note for parent: Help your child to work with numbers by saying a number and asking them what number is one more/less.

Count the objects in the big picture.
Write the correct number in each box.

Note for parent: To help find the totals, your child can mark each object as they count.

Comparing

Colour most spaceships red. Colour the rest of the spaceships blue. Write the numbers in the boxes.

red spaceships

blue spaceships

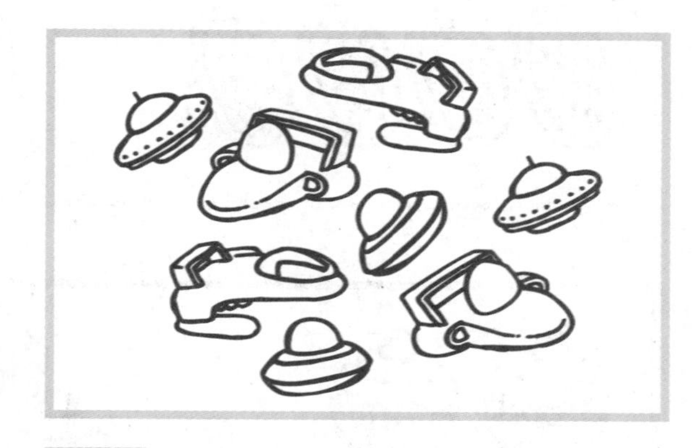

red spaceships

blue spaceships

red spaceships

blue spaceships

spaceships altogether

red spaceships

blue spaceships

spaceships altogether

Note for parent: Your child can choose the number of spaceships to colour red, but there must be more red spaceships than blue ones.

Putting together

Count each set. Write how many there are altogether.

biscuits altogether

cakes altogether

pizzas altogether

ice creams altogether

sweets altogether

Note for parent: Encourage your child to count on from the first number to find the total.

Count the spots on each monster.
How many spots are there altogether?

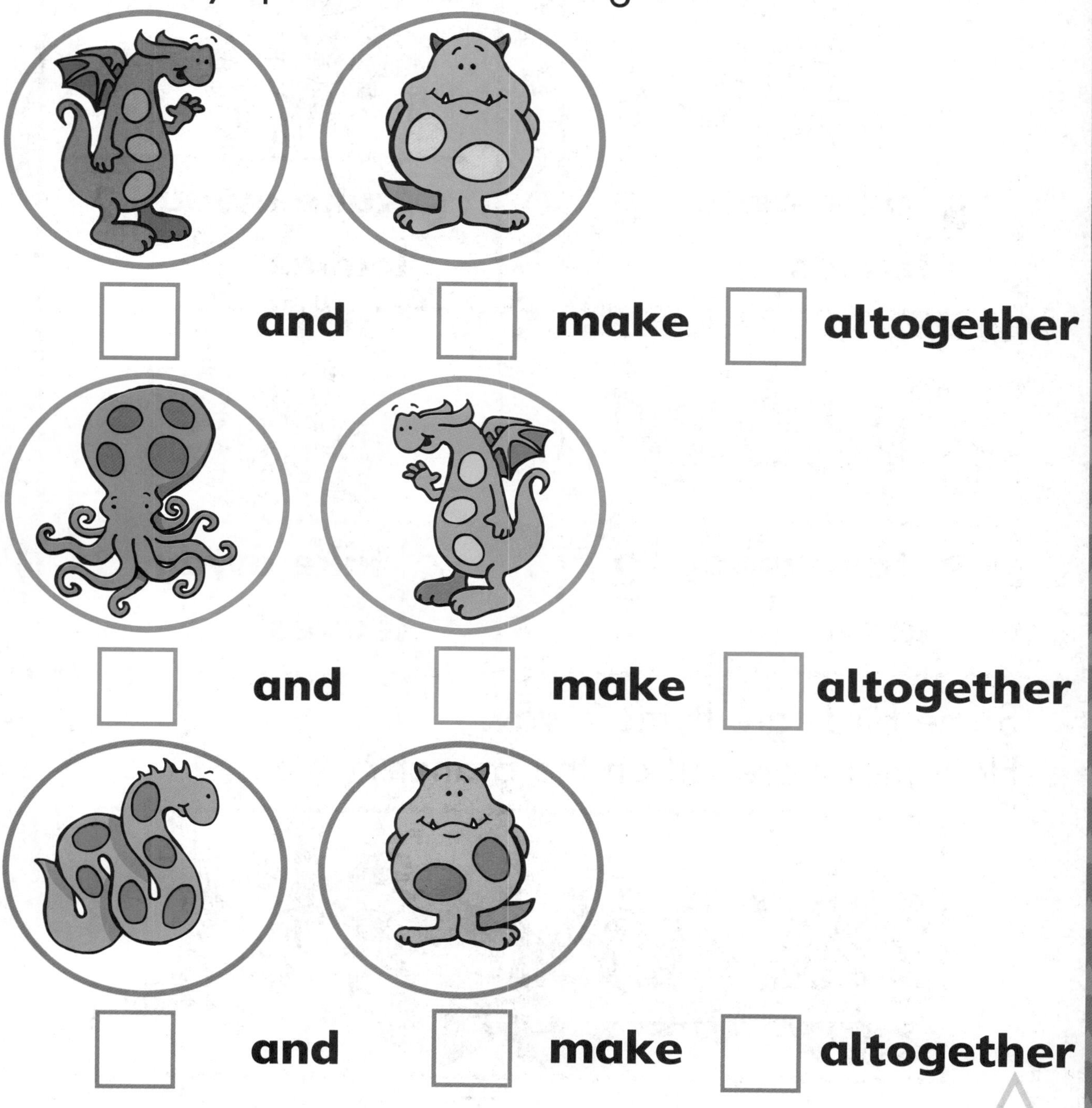

☐ and ☐ make ☐ altogether

☐ and ☐ make ☐ altogether

☐ and ☐ make ☐ altogether

How many are left?

Cross out two in each set. Write how many are left.

5 **take away** 2
leaves ☐

6 **take away** 2
leaves ☐

8 **take away** 2
leaves ☐

4 **take away** 2
leaves ☐

Some birds are flying away.
How many are left on the branch?

9 **take away** 3 **leaves** ☐

Note for parent: This activity will help your child begin to understand the idea of taking away (subtracting).

Finding differences

How many more children are there than chairs?

children

chairs

difference →

children

chairs

difference →

children

chairs

difference →

Note for parent: Finding the difference is the same as counting up from the smaller number to the larger one.

Number machines

Sweets go into these adding machines.
Write how many come out of each machine.

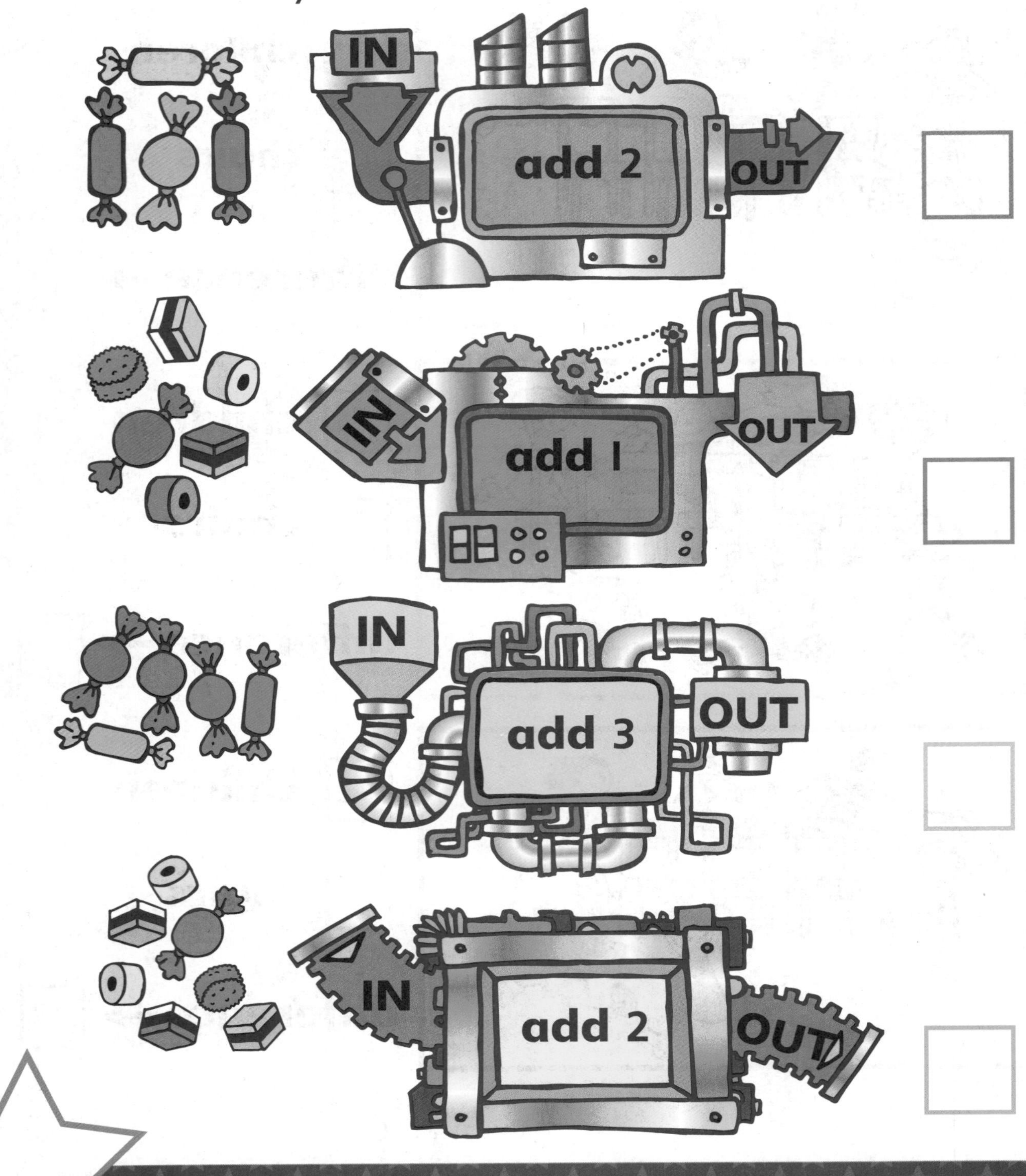

Note for parent: Encourage your child to count on from the IN number for adding, and to count back for taking away.

Drinks go into these take-away machines.
Write how many come out of each machine.

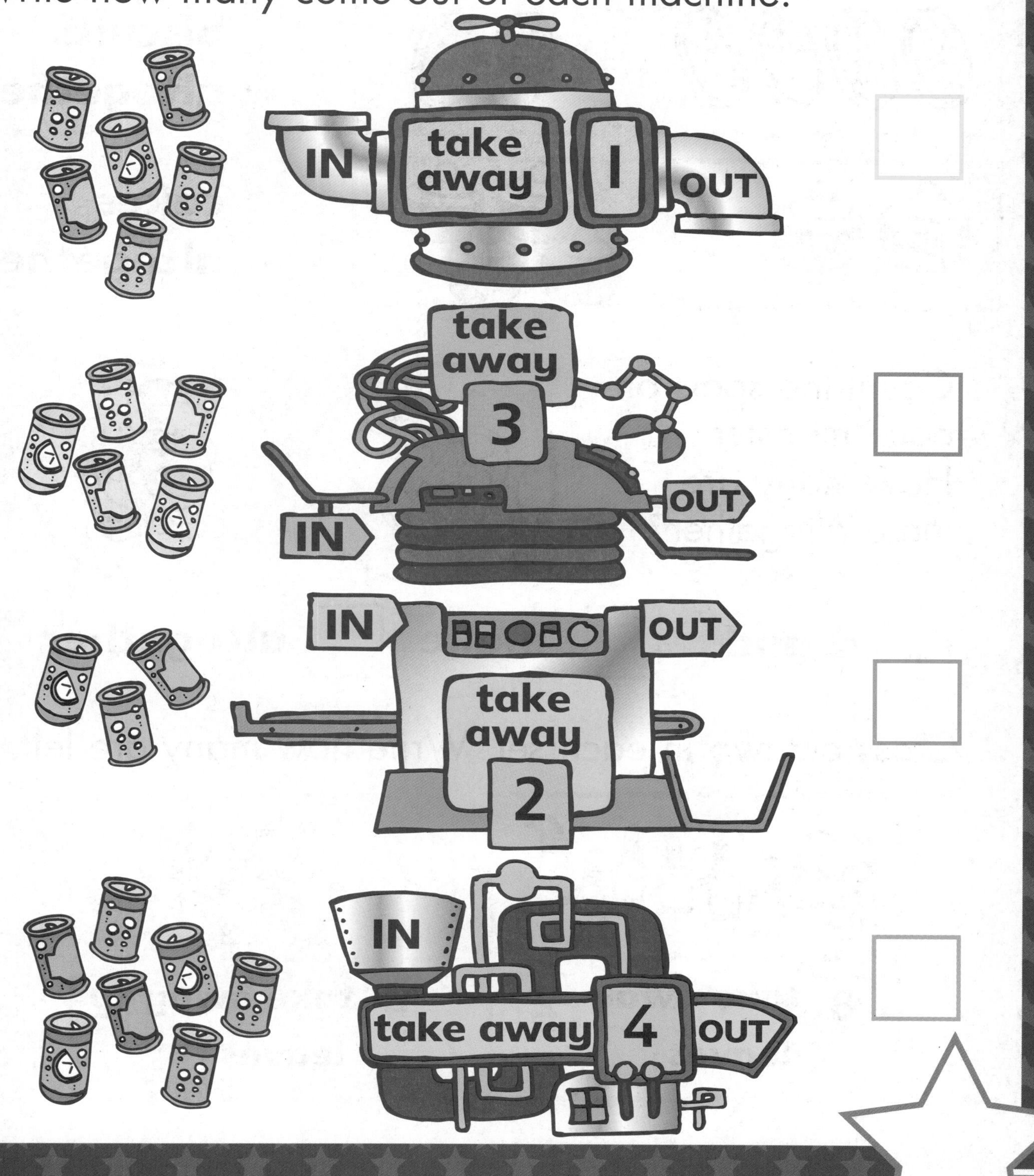

Quick quiz

Count each set. Write how many there are altogether.

☐ **biscuits altogether**

☐ **cakes altogether**

Count the spots on each monster. How many are there altogether?

☐ **and** ☐ **make** ☐ **altogether**

Cross out two in each set. Write how many are left.

8 take away 2 leaves ☐

4 take away 2 leaves ☐

Note for parent: This page helps to find out what your child can remember.

Numbers to 20

Join each word to a number.

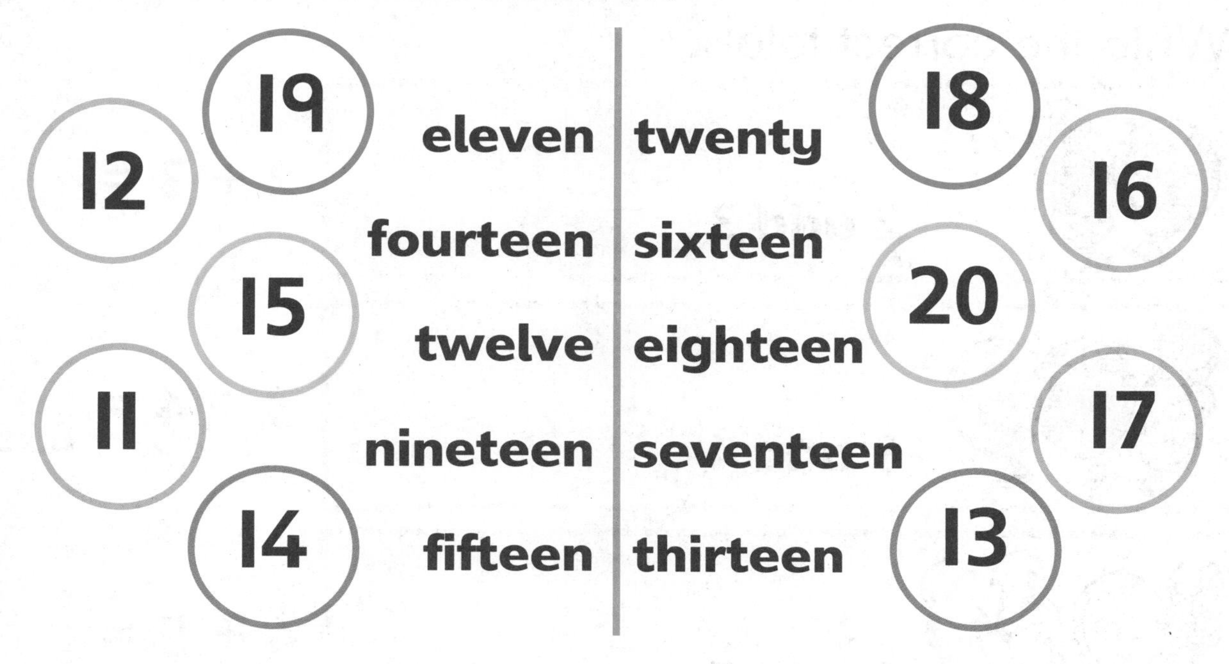

Complete the number table.

eleven	**11**
	12
thirteen	
fourteen	
	15
sixteen	
	17
	18
nineteen	
	20

Group the numbers by their colour circles above.

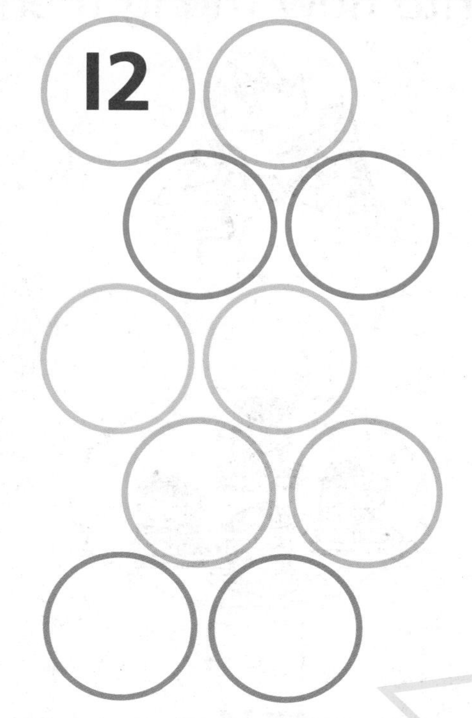

Note for parent: Solving problems using tables and sorting numbers using different criteria for grouping them are important maths skills for your child at this age.

Adding

Draw the extra balloons in each row.
Write the correct totals.

2 add 3

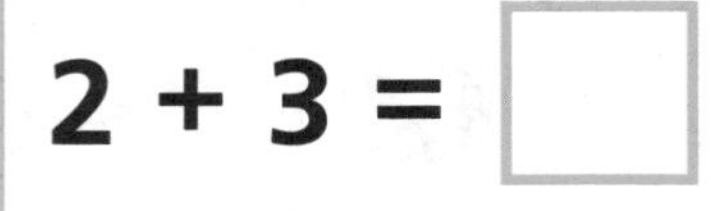

2 + 3 = ☐

3 add 4

3 + 4 = ☐

4 add 5

4 + 5 = ☐

Write how many there are altogether.

☐ **+** ☐ **=** ☐

☐ **+** ☐ **=** ☐

Note for parent: Ask your child what the addition sign (+) and the equals sign (=) mean. This will help them to recognize and use the signs correctly.

Write how many coloured pencils there are altogether.

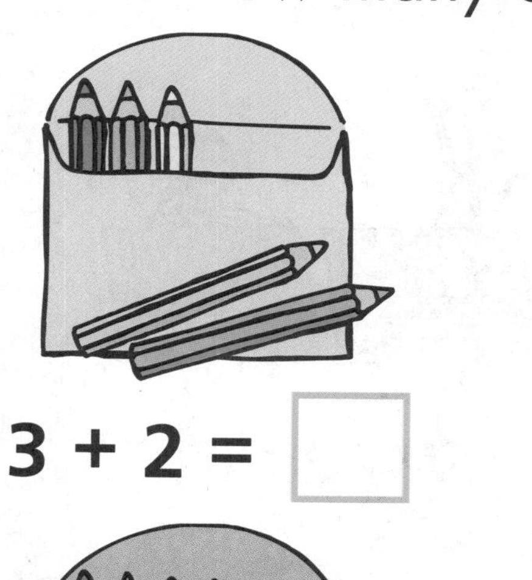

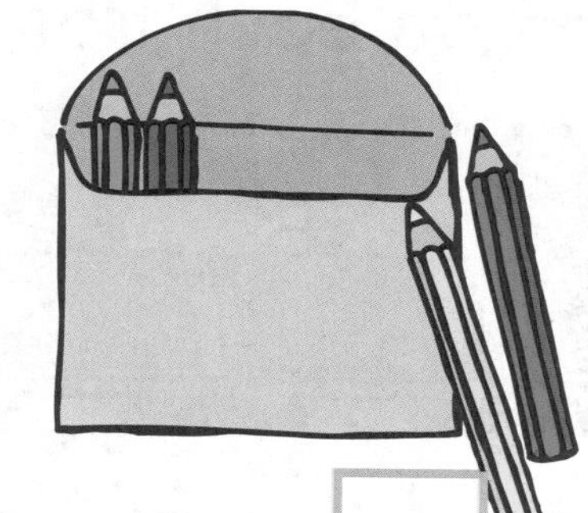

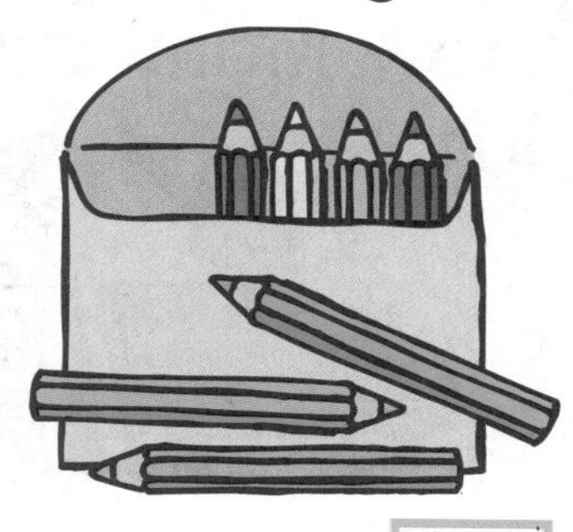

3 + 2 = ☐

2 + 2 = ☐

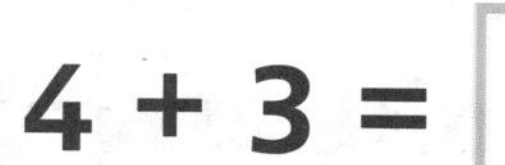

4 + 3 = ☐

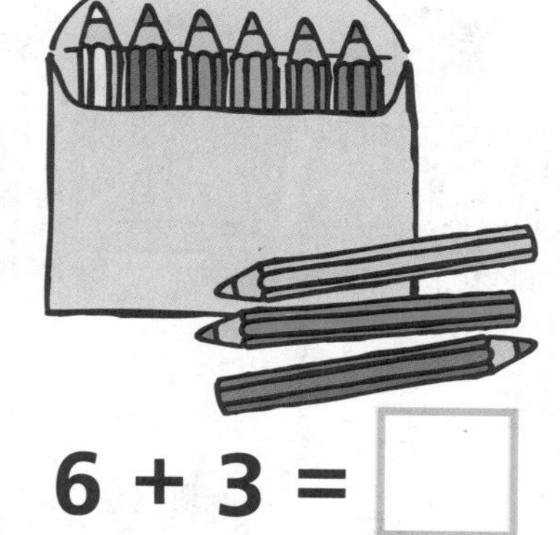

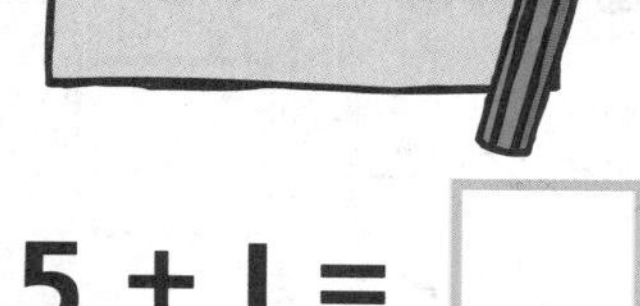

5 + 1 = ☐

6 + 3 = ☐

4 + 5 = ☐

Join each sum to the correct total.

Taking away

Two children get out of each of these trains.
How many are left on each train?

7 take away 2 is ☐

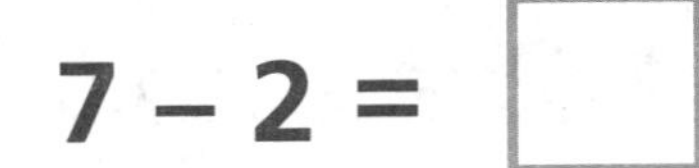

7 – 2 = ☐

5 take away 2 is ☐

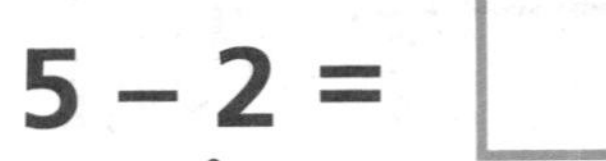

5 – 2 = ☐

8 take away 2 is ☐ **8 – 2 =** ☐

Cross out some flags. Write how many are left.

9 – ☐ **is** ☐

Note for parent: Use the words 'subtract' and 'take away' with your child to help them to recognize and understand the subtraction sign (–).

Draw how many balls come out of the machines.
Write the totals in the red boxes.

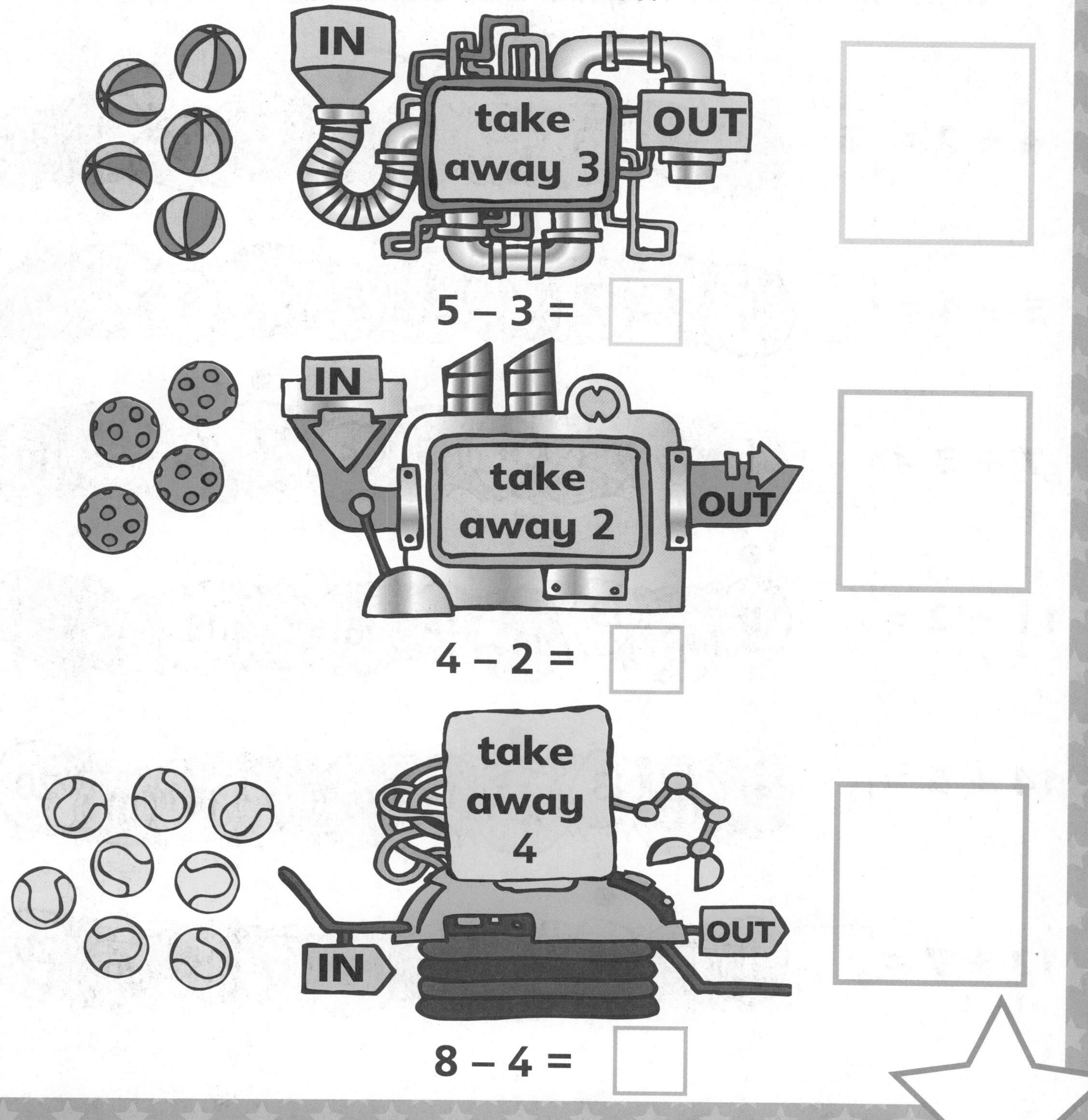

Counting on

Use the number track to count on. Show the jumps and write the answer. The first one has been done for you.

4 + 2 = 6

1 2 3 4 5 6 7 8 9 10

5 + 4 = ☐

1 2 3 4 5 6 7 8 9 10

7 + 3 = ☐

1 2 3 4 5 6 7 8 9 10

11 + 2 = ☐

11 12 13 14 15 16 17 18 19 20

14 + 5 = ☐

11 12 13 14 15 16 17 18 19 20

13 + 7 = ☐

11 12 13 14 15 16 17 18 19 20

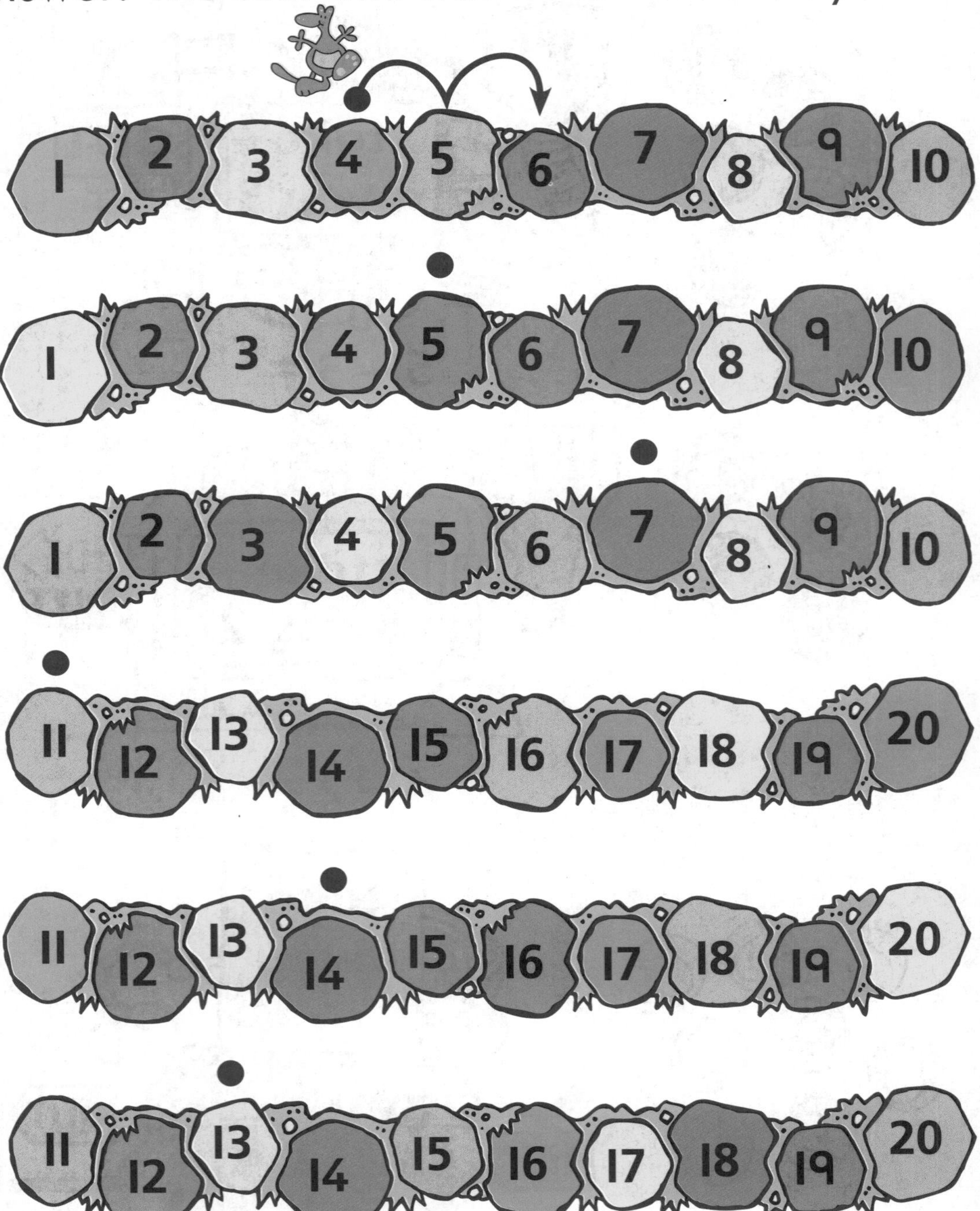

Note for parent: This activity introduces adding to two-digit numbers. Encourage your child to count on in twos and fives along each number track.

Join each rocket to the correct answer on the number track.

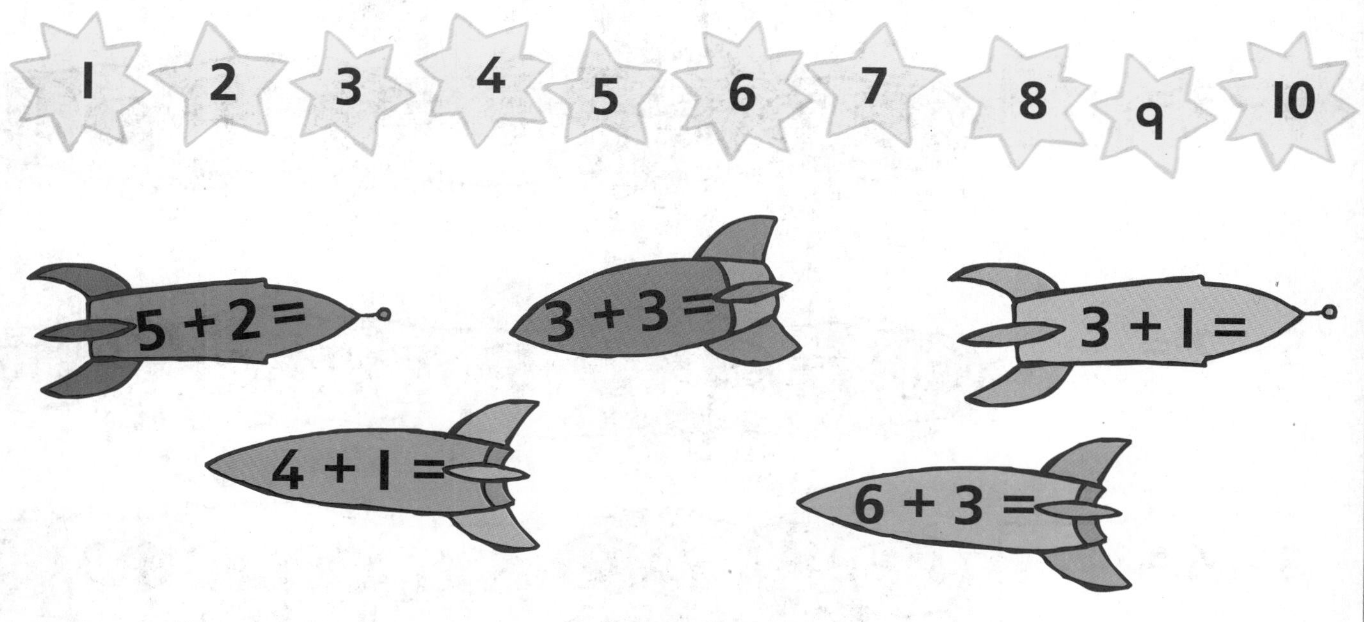

Write the missing numbers in these counting patterns.

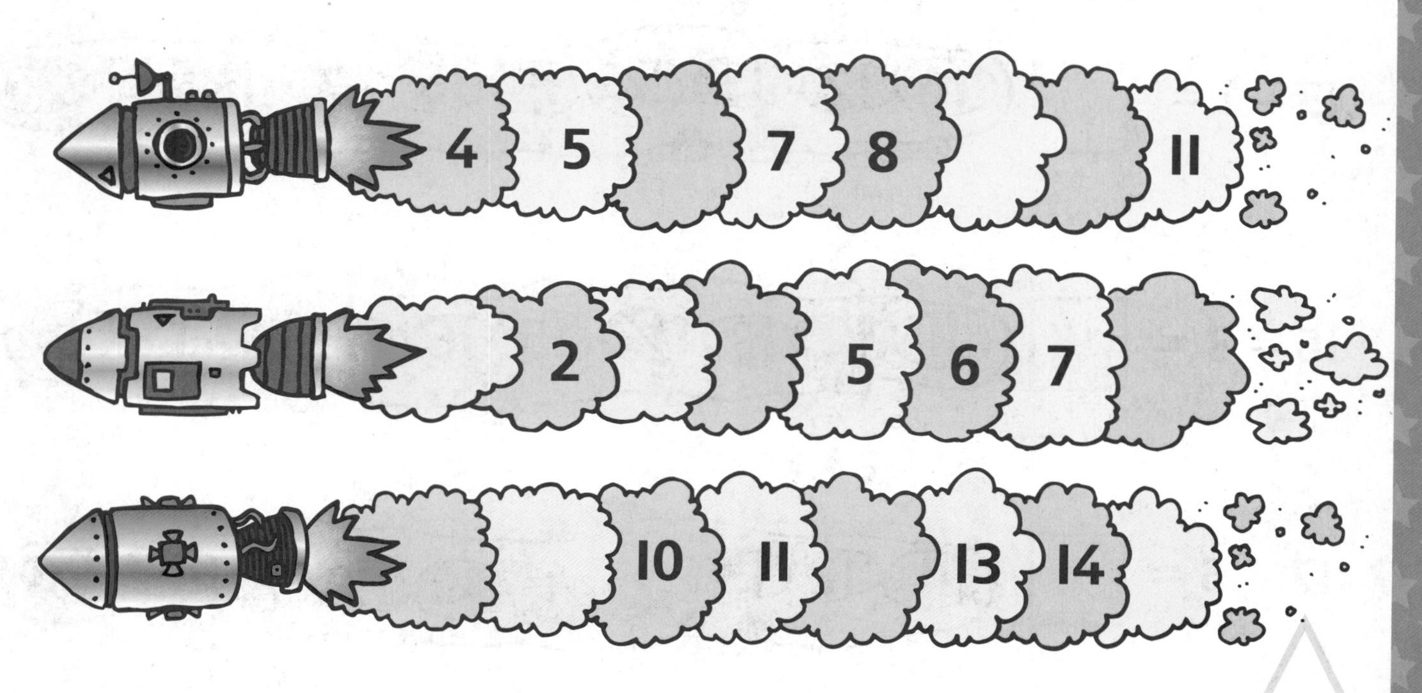

Counting back

Use the number track to count back. Show the jumps and write the answer.

6 – 3 = ☐

5 – 2 = ☐

8 – 4 = ☐

13 – 1 = ☐

16 – 3 = ☐

17 – 6 = ☐

Note for parent: This activity introduces subtracting from two-digit numbers. Encourage your child to count back in twos and fives along each number track.

Work out each answer. Colour the correct number in the number track to match.

Addition bonds

Make these totals in different ways.
Write the answers in the boxes.

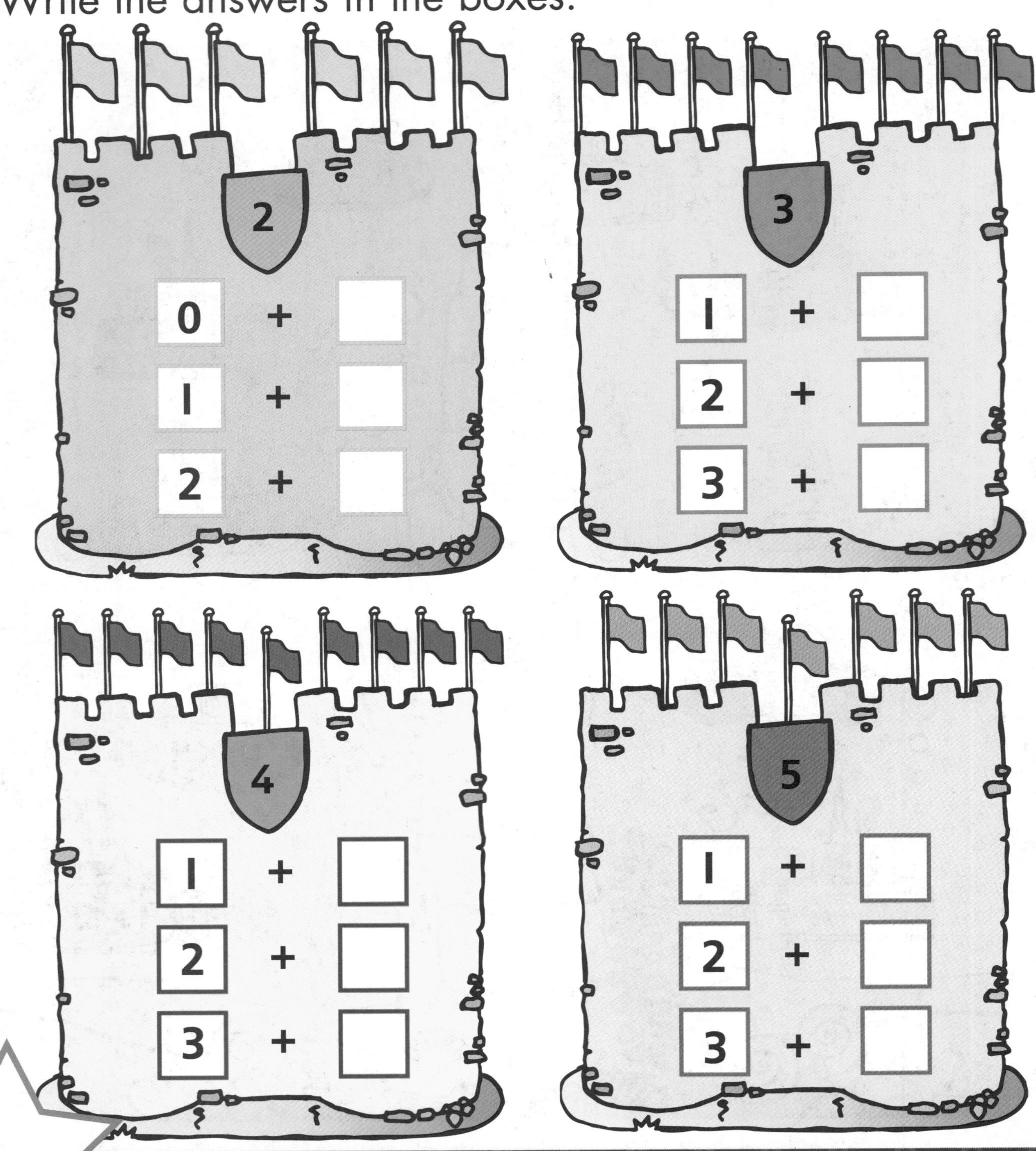

Note for parent: This activity helps your child to understand that numbers can be added in any order to achieve the same total. For example, 2 + 3 = 3 + 2 = 5.

Draw a line from each flower to the pot with the correct total.

What can you see if you colour all the shapes with a total of 10?

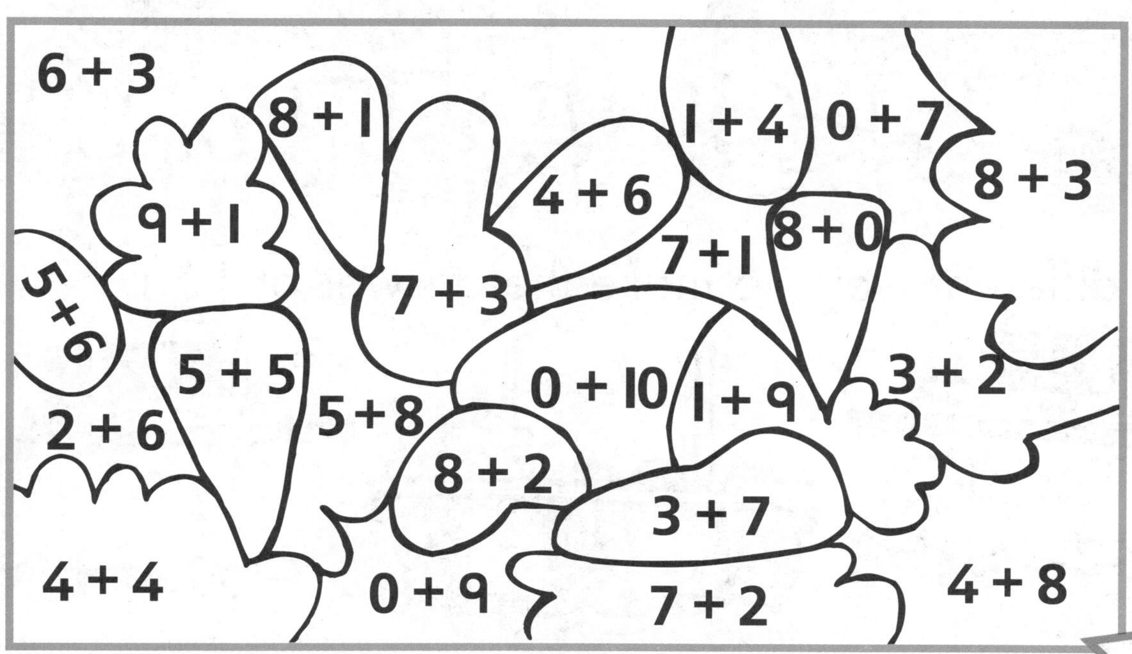

Subtraction bonds

Find different ways of making 1 and 2.

Find different ways to make the answer of 5.

Note for parent: Subtraction bonds with totals up to five and pairs with a total of ten are key learning objectives for your child in this age group.

Quick quiz

Join the sums to the correct totals.

Draw how many balls come out of the machines.

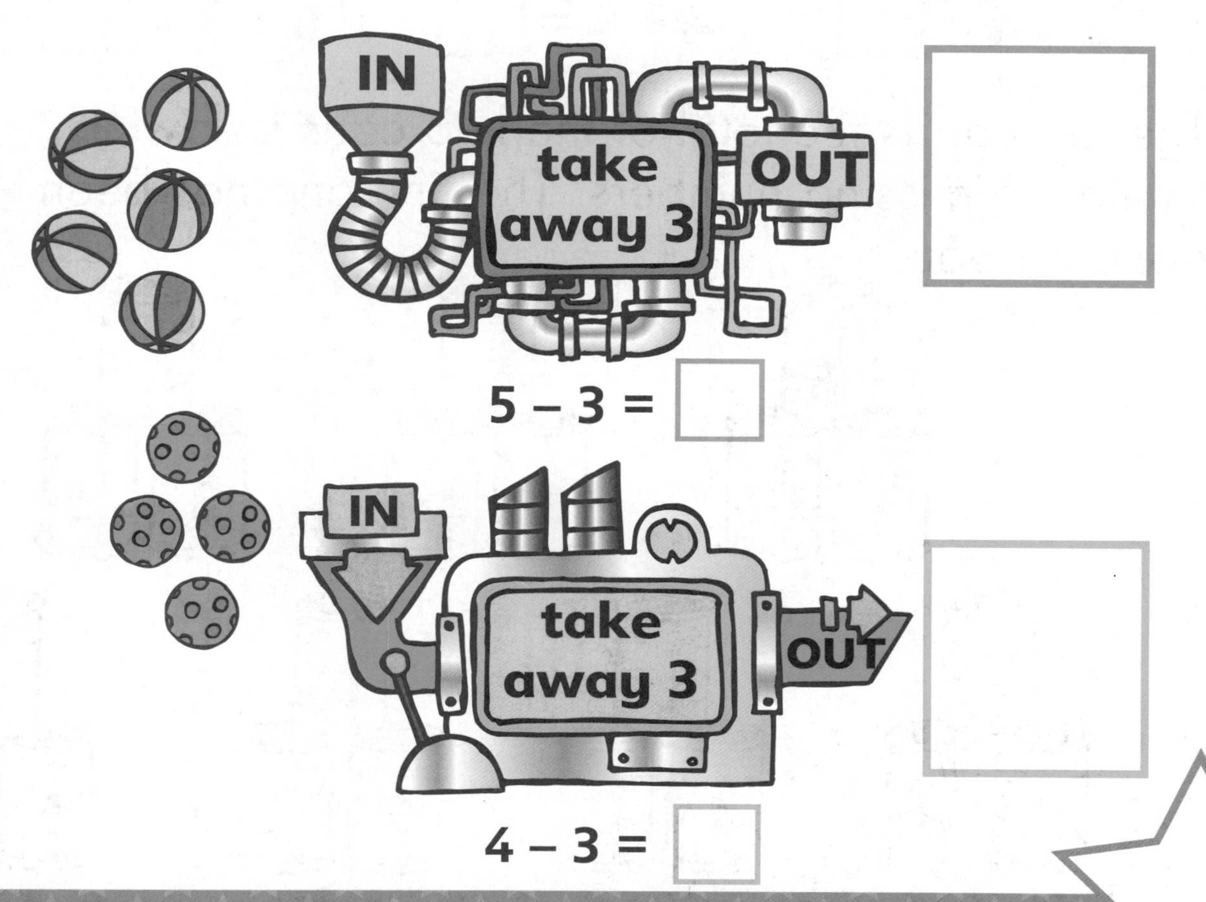

Addition practice

Write the answers in the boxes. Use the number track to help you.

4 + 3 = ☐ 6 + 2 = ☐ 5 + 5 = ☐

9 + 1 = ☐ 7 + 2 = ☐ 3 + 5 = ☐

2 + 4 = ☐ 4 + 4 = ☐ 6 + 3 = ☐

The top can is the total of the two cans below. Write the missing numbers. The first one has been done for you.

Note for parent: On a separate piece of paper, ask your child to write out as sums the addition facts shown on the tin cans, using the + and = symbols they have learned.

Write the missing numbers.

___ + 2 = 4 ___ + 3 = 6 4 + ___ = 8

5 + ___ = 10 ___ + 8 = 10 6 + ___ = 10

___ + 7 = 10 1 + ___ = 10 ___ + 0 = 10

Follow these trails to reach 10.
Write the missing totals.

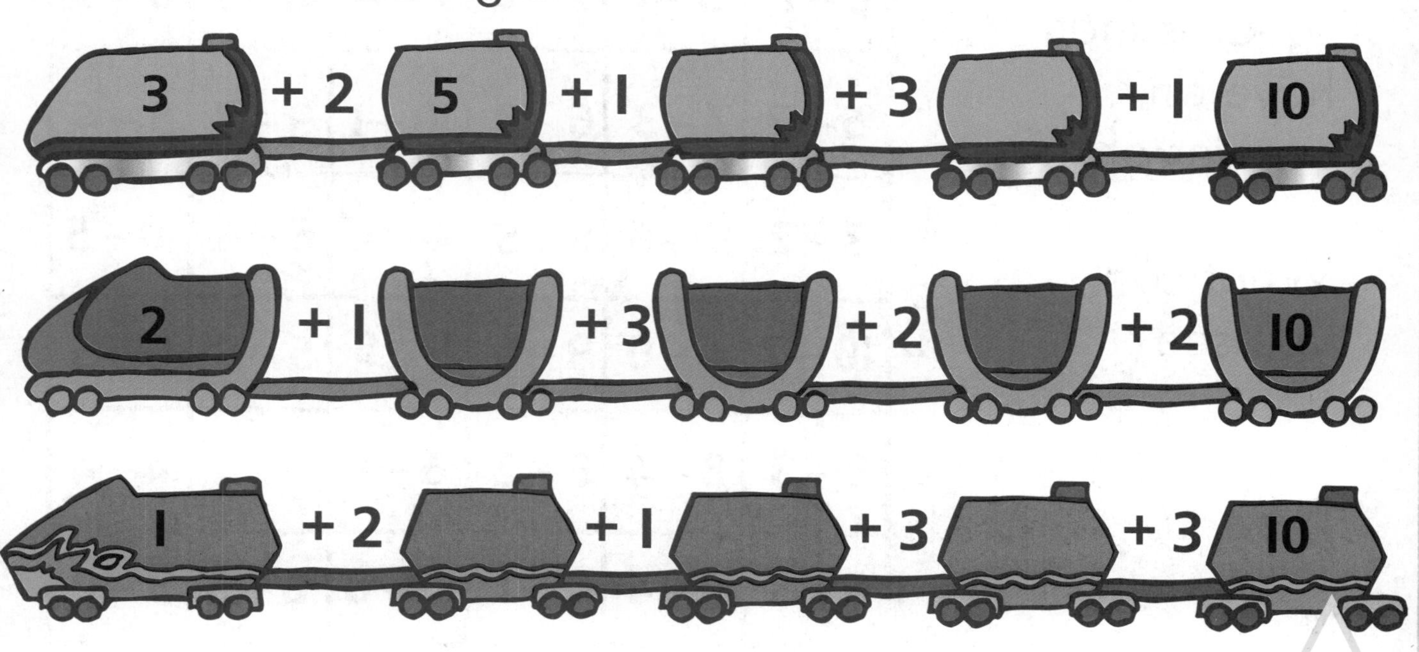

Subtraction practice

Write the answers in the boxes. Use the number track to help you.

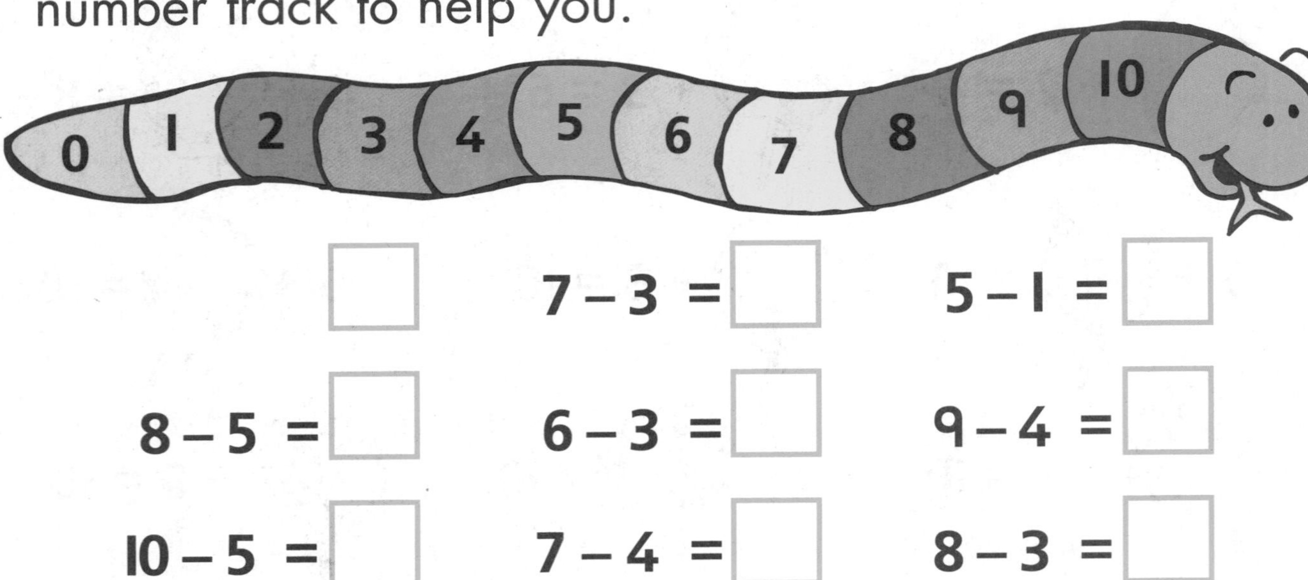

$\square$ $\quad 7 - 3 = \square$ $\quad 5 - 1 = \square$

$8 - 5 = \square$ $\quad 6 - 3 = \square$ $\quad 9 - 4 = \square$

$10 - 5 = \square$ $\quad 7 - 4 = \square$ $\quad 8 - 3 = \square$

Colour the squares that have an answer of 4.

What can you see?

6 – 1	5 – 1	7 – 2	7 – 4	8 – 2	8 – 3
5 – 2	7 – 3	6 – 3	10 – 1	9 – 7	5 – 4
3 – 2	10 – 6	8 – 5	4 – 4	6 – 4	10 – 5
10 – 7	4 – 0	9 – 6	9 – 5	5 – 0	6 – 5
8 – 3	8 – 4	6 – 2	5 – 1	7 – 3	4 – 4
5 – 3	9 – 4	7 – 1	10 – 6	8 – 6	3 – 0

Note for parent: On a separate piece of paper, ask your child to write out the subtractions shown in the squares and include the answers, using the – and = symbols they have learned.

Write the missing numbers.

⬡ − 5 = 5 ▲ − 4 = 4 ● − 3 = 3

4 − ⬣ = 2 10 − ⯃ = 4 10 − ■ = 8

▯ − 3 = 7 ⏢ − 8 = 2 10 − ✶ = 1

Draw a line to join each pair of stars with the same answer.

4 − 3 8 − 5 9 − 7

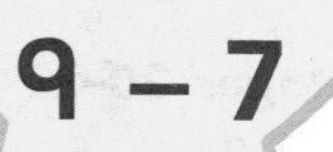

10 − 3 9 − 2

7 − 4 6 − 4 7 − 6

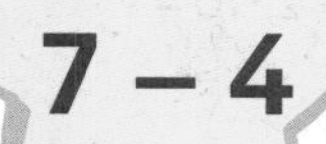

Answers

Pages 4–5

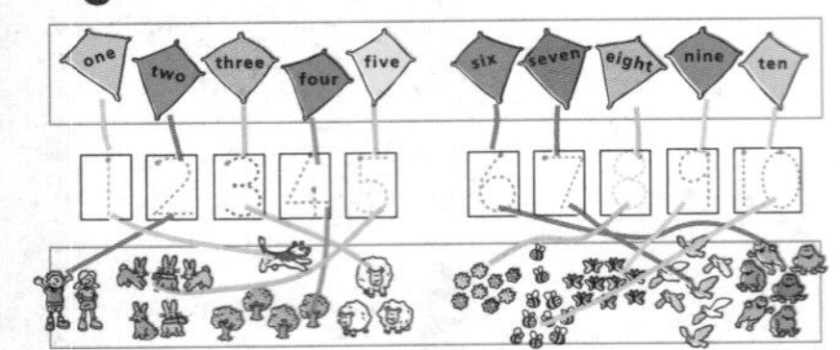

Page 6

Page 7

There should be more spaceships coloured red than blue in each box. 9 spaceships altogether, 10 spaceships altogether.

Pages 8–9

6 biscuits altogether, 6 cakes altogether, 5 pizzas altogether, 7 ice creams altogether, 9 sweets altogether.
3 and 2 make 5 altogether, 4 and 3 make 7 altogether, 6 and 2 make 8 altogether.

Page 10

5 take away 2 leaves 3, 6 take away 2 leaves 4, 8 take away 2 leaves 6, 4 take away 2 leaves 2, 9 take away 3 leaves 6.

Page 11

5 children, 4 chairs, difference = 1.
7 children, 5 chairs, difference = 2.
6 children, 3 chairs, difference = 3.

Pages 12–13

4 sweets add 2 sweets = 6 sweets,
6 sweets add 1 sweet = 7 sweets,
5 sweets add 3 sweets = 8 sweets,
7 sweets add 2 sweets = 9 sweets.
6 drinks take away 1 drink = 5 drinks,
5 drinks take away 3 drinks = 2 drinks,
3 drinks take away 2 drinks = 1 drink,
7 drinks take away 4 drinks = 3 drinks.

Page 14

6 biscuits altogether, 6 cakes altogether.
6 and 2 make 8 altogether.
8 take away 2 leaves 6,
4 take away 2 leaves 2.

Page 15

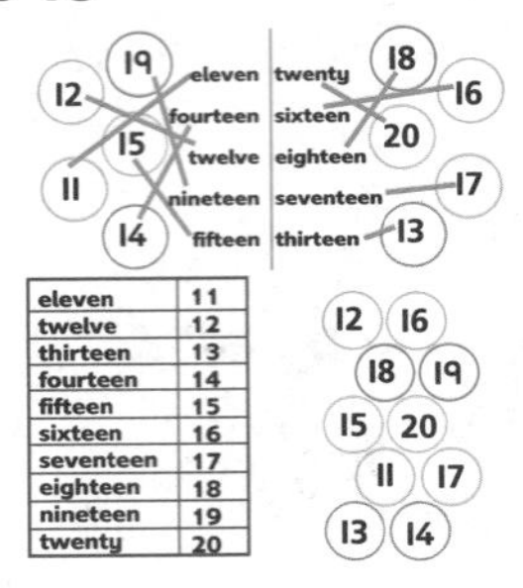

eleven	11
twelve	12
thirteen	13
fourteen	14
fifteen	15
sixteen	16
seventeen	17
eighteen	18
nineteen	19
twenty	20

Pages 16–17

2 + 3 = 5, 3 + 4 = 7, 4 + 5 = 9.
3 + 5 = 8 altogether, 4 + 2 = 6 altogether. 3 + 2 = 5, 2 + 2 = 4, 4 + 3 = 7, 5 + 1 = 6, 6 + 3 = 9, 4 + 5 = 9.

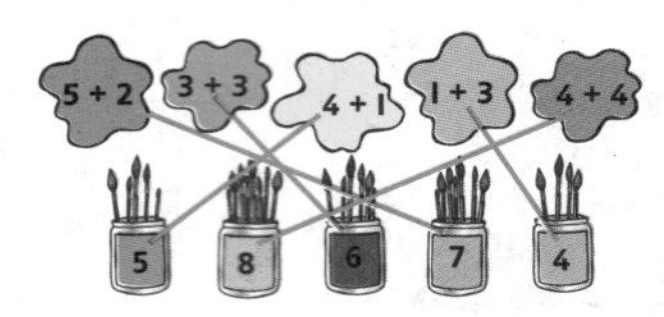

Pages 18–19

7 – 2 = 5, 5 – 2 = 3, 8 – 2 = 6.
Parents need to check child's answer for the last sum on page 18.
5 balls take away 3 balls = 2 balls, 4 balls take away 2 balls = 2 balls, 8 balls take away 4 balls = 4 balls.

Pages 20–21

4 + 2 = 6, 5 + 4 = 9, 7 + 3 = 10, 11 + 2 = 13, 14 + 5 =19, 13 + 7 = 20.
5 + 2 = 7, 4 + 1 = 5, 3 + 3 = 6, 6 + 3 = 9, 3 + 1 = 4.
The missing numbers are:
blue rocket – 6, 9, 10; green rocket – 1, 3, 4, 8; red rocket – 8, 9, 12, 15.

Pages 22–23

6 – 3 = 3, 5 – 2 = 3, 8 – 4 = 4, 13 – 1 = 12, 16 – 3 = 13, 17 – 6 = 11.

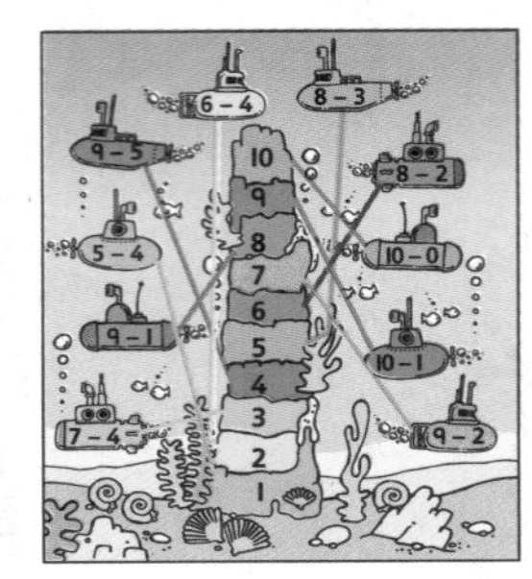

Pages 24–25

2: 0 + 2, 1 + 1, 2 + 0. 3: 1 + 2, 2 + 1, 3 + 0. 4: 1 + 3, 2 + 2, 3 + 1. 5: 1 + 4, 2 + 3, 3 + 2.

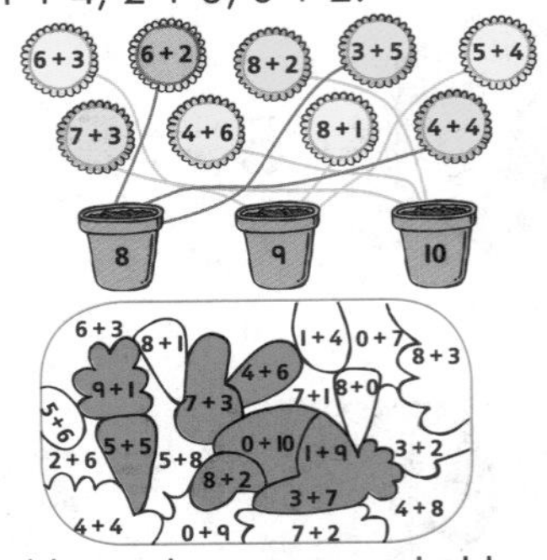

A rabbit and a carrot are hidden among the shapes.

Page 26

1: 2 – 1, 3 – 2, 4 – 3, 5 – 4, 10 – 9.
2: 5 – 3, 4 – 2, 3 – 1, 2 – 0, 10 – 8.
Possible answers include: 6 – 1, 7 – 2, 8 – 3, 9 – 4.

Page 27

5 + 2 = 7, 4 + 1 = 5, 4 + 4 = 8.
5 balls take away 3 balls = 2 balls,
4 balls take away 3 balls = 1 ball.

Pages 28–29

4 + 3 = 7, 6 + 2 = 8, 5 + 5 = 10, 9 + 1 = 10, 7 + 2 = 9, 3 + 5 = 8, 2 + 4 = 6, 4 + 4 = 8, 6 + 3 = 9.
Missing numbers:
row 1: 6, 8; row 2: 10, 9, 8, 10.
2 + 2 = 4, 3 + 3 = 6, 4 + 4 = 8, 5 + 5 = 10, 2 + 8 = 10, 6 + 4 = 10, 3 + 7 = 10, 1 + 9 = 10, 10 + 0 = 10.
Missing totals: green train: 6, 9; purple train: 3, 6, 8; red train: 3, 4, 7.

Pages 30–31

6 – 4 = 2, 7 – 3 = 4, 5 – 1 = 4, 8 – 5 = 3, 6 – 3 = 3, 9 – 4 = 5, 10 – 5 = 5, 7 – 4 = 3, 8 – 3 = 5.

The number 4 is hidden in the grid.

10 – 5 = 5, 8 – 4 = 4, 6 – 3 = 3, 4 – 2 = 2, 10 – 6 = 4, 10 – 2 = 8, 10 – 3 = 7, 10 – 8 = 2, 10 – 9 = 1.